International Journal for Religious Freedom (IJRF)
Journal of the International Institute for Religious Freedom

The IJRF aims to provide a platform for scholarly discourse on religious freedom and persecution. It is an interdisciplinary, international, peer reviewed journal, serving the dissemination of new research on religious freedom and contains research articles, documentation, book reviews, academic news and other relevant items.

The editors welcome the submission of any contribution to the journal. Manuscripts submitted for publication are assessed by a panel of referees and the decision to publish is dependent on their reports. The IJRF is listed on the DoHET "Approved list of South African journals" and subscribes to the Code of Best Practice in Scholarly Journal Publishing, Editing and Peer Review of 2018 as well as the National Code of Best Practice in Editorial Discretion and Peer Review for South African Scholarly Journals and the supplementary Guidelines for Best Practice of the Forum of Editors of Academic Law Journals in South Africa.

The IJRF is freely available online: www.iirf.eu, as a paid print subscription, and via SABINET.

Editorial Committee

Editors	Prof Dr Christof Sauer, Cape Town, South Africa	editor@iirf.eu
	Prof Dr Thomas Schirrmacher, Bonn, Germany	
Managing Editor	Prof Dr Janet Epp Buckingham	
	(LLD Stellenbosch University), Ottawa, Canada	editor@iirf.eu
Book Reviews	Dr Werner Nicolaas Nel, Johannesburg, South Africa	bookreviews@iirf.eu
Noteworthy	vacant	noteworthy@iirf.eu

Editorial Board

Prof Dr P Coertzen, Stellenbosch, South Africa
Prof Dr R Velosso Ewell, Londrina, Brazil
Prof S A de Freitas, Bloemfontein, South Africa
Prof Dr L Fernandez, Cape Town, South Africa
Prof Dr K Gnanakan, Shillong/Bangalore, India
Dr B Intan, Jakarta, Indonesia
Prof Dr T K Johnson, Prague, Czech Republic
Drs B Konutgan, Istanbul, Turkey
Dr P Marshall, Washington DC, USA

Prof Dr Dr J W Montgomery, Straßbourg, France
Rev P Netha, Bulawayo, Zimbabwe
Prof Dr A Ojacor, Kampala, Uganda
Prof Dr B J G Reitsma, Amsterdam, Netherlands
Prof Dr R Rothfuss, Tübingen, Germany
Prof Dr C Schirrmacher, Bonn, Germany
Prof Dr D L Stults, Oklahoma, USA
Prof Dr J P J Theron †, Pretoria, South Africa

Subscriptions 2016

Annual subscription fee:
SA Rand 300
VAT and postage included.
See subscription form in the back.

For international payments use:
http://iirfct.givengain.org
(pay in Rand!)

Bank details
Beneficiary: International Institute for Religious Freedom, Cape Town · Bank: Standard Bank · Branch: Sea Point
Branch Code: 02 41 09 · Account Number: 071 117 431
SWIFT Code: SBZAZAJJ

IJRF · P.O. Box 1336 · Sun Valley 7985 · Rep South Africa
editor@iirf.eu

International Institute for Religious Freedom (IIRF)
of the World Evangelical Alliance

www.iirf.eu

Friedrichstr. 38
2nd Floor
53111 Bonn
Germany
Bonn@iirf.eu

PO Box
Sun Val
Cape To
South A
CapeTow

International Journal for Religious Freedom
Volume 9, Issue 1/2, 2016

ISSN 2070-5484
ISBN 978-3-86269-209-5

Articles and opinions published in IJRF do not necessarily reflect the views of the editors, of IIRF or of the sponsors.

© Copyright 2016 is with the individual authors or bodies mentioned in the respective items. Printed with permission.

Acknowledgement of Sponsors
We would like to thank the sponsors who supported the editing, printing and distribution of this issue of IJRF. Their views and opinions are not necessarily those of IIRF and vice versa.
- Evangelical Lutheran Church in Württemberg, Germany www.elk-wue.de/landeskirche/international-information-en/
- Gebende Häude (Giving Hands), www.gebende-haende.de

Subscribe to get IJRF via email (time delayed – 1 March; 1 September)

➢ To receive new issues of IJRF electronically on release, send an email to: subscribe-ijrf-fulltext-subscribe@bucer.eu

➢ To receive an email notice about a new issue of IJRF available online, send an email to: subscribe-ijrf-notice-subscribe@bucer.eu

---

Note to librarians: IJRF is also available as an ePublication from Sabinet (www.sabinet.co.za). The first full volume of IJRF appeared in 2009. There was only one pilot issue in 2008.

Typesetting: Ben Nimmo (Solid Ground), www.solidground.training

Cover art: Aisha
Photo credit: Open Doors International
This is a self-portrait of Aisha, created during a workshop organized by Open Doors for healing from trauma. Aisha is a Nigerian who suffered sexual violence, at the hands of either militant Fulani herdsmen or the Islamic extremist group Boko Haram. The Open Doors workshop seeks to affirm and empower women like Aisha. Incorporating local fabric, they experienced affirmation of their identity as Nigerian women and were also reminded of their value as daughters of God. For more details, see https://www.opendoorsca.org/tears-of-gold/.

Contents

International Journal for Religious Freedom
Volume 9, Issue 1/2, 2016
ISSN 2070-5484

Editorial 5

In my opinion

The journey to a Gender and Religious Freedom Network
Emma Dipper 9

The restricted legal status of women: An inconvenience for Christian women or a vulnerability for the church?
Olivia Jackson 17

Articles

"There is neither male nor female": Theological reflection on Galatians 3:28 as a faith-based response to gender-specific persecution
Samuel Oluwatosin Okanlawon 25

Assessing the specificity of the vulnerability of girls and women belonging to religious minorities: A methodological exploration
Dennis P. Petri 35

Left behind: An analysis of the United Nations' response to the intersecting identities of gender and religion
Rebecca Symes 49

At the crossroads of freedom of religion and women's equality rights: Some reflections from South Asia
Saumya Uma 67

Strengthening resilience among women from Christian minorities: The Strength2Stand approach
Rachel 81

Christian women facing persecution in India: A review and recommendations
Jayakumar Ramachandran 91

Noteworthy 107

Book Reviews 111

Guidelines for authors 119
Subscriptions 122

International Journal for Religious Freedom (IJRF)

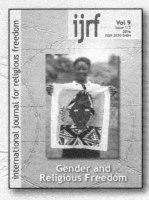

Journal of the International Institute for Religious Freedom
ISSN 2070-5484

IJRF is published twice annually and aims to provide a platform for scholarly discourse on religious freedom in general and the persecution of Christians in particular. It is an interdisciplinary, international, peer reviewed journal, serving the dissemination of new research on religious freedom and contains research articles, documentation, book reviews, academic news and other relevant items.

The editors welcome the submission of any contribution to the journal. Manuscripts submitted for publication are assessed by a panel of referees and the decision to publish is dependent on their reports.

Editorial Committee

Editors	Prof Dr Thomas Schirrmacher, Bonn, Germany
	Prof Dr Christof Sauer, Cape Town, South Africa
Managing Editor	Prof Dr Janet Epp Buckingham, Ottawa, Canada

Free electronic subscription (time delayed):

- To receive new issues of IJRF electronically on release (1 MB), send an email to:
  subscribe-ijrf-fulltext-subscribe@bucer.eu

- To receive an email notice only about a new issue of IJRF available online, send an email to:
  subscribe-ijrf-notice-subscribe@bucer.eu

Paid subscriptions 2016
Annual subscription fee
for 2 issues:
South African Rand 300
VAT and postage included

IJRF · P.O. Box 1336 · Sun Valley 7985 · Rep South Africa
editor@iirf.eu

w w w . i i r f . e u

Editorial

Special issue on gender and persecution

Religious persecution is frequently gender-specific, impacting men and women differently. Grassroots research in countries such as Egypt and Pakistan in 2012 and 2013 showed that many women were experiencing double vulnerability not only due to their faith, but also as women. As a result, representatives of international charities who aid Christians facing persecution decided to form a steering group, bringing together non-governmental agencies, Christian ministries, and church leaders who were already seeking to address these issues.[1]

The first consultation was held in Marcham, near Oxford, UK in March 2016 with the topic of "Women and Persecution." The practitioners and academics who participated in the event issued a "Message to the Global Church on the Double Vulnerability of Women due to Gender and Religion".[2]

As a follow-up, a much larger consultation was held in June 2017 at the Evangelische Theologische Faculteit in Leuven, Belgium, now framing the topic as "Christian Women under Pressure for Their Faith"[3] and issuing a "Leuven Letter." This consultation had a dedicated scholarly track[4] conducted parallel to other working groups.

In 2019, during the gender and religious freedom consultation in Abuja, Nigeria, another scholarly track was offered.

Our guest editor for this special issue on gender and persecution is Peirong Lin, PhD, the Human Resource Director and Research Coordinator for the World Evangelical Alliance's Department for Theological Concerns in Bonn, Germany. Peirong, a native of Singapore, has studied at university institutions on three

---

[1] The consultation was organized by Release Women, an integral part of Release International, in collaboration with the International Institute for Religious Freedom (IIRF) and the Religious Liberty Partnership.

[2] See "Message to the Global Church on the Double Vulnerability of Women due to Gender and Religion." (2017). In T. Johnson, T. Schirrmacher and C. Sauer (eds.), Global Statements on Freedom of Religion or Belief, 115–17. Bonn: Culture and Science Publishing: Available at https://www.iirf.eu/journal-books/global-issues-series/global-declarations-on-freedom-of-religion-or-belief-and-human-rights/.

[3] An important new partner in the organisation of the consultation was the women's ministry of Open Doors International. Their research can be found at www.opendoorsanalytical.org (password: freedom). See also Fisher, Helene, Elizabeth Lane Miller and Christof Sauer (2020). "Wounded because of religion: Identifying the components of gender-specific religious persecution of Christians." Mission Studies: Locating European Missions in a Wounded World in Deep Transformation. 37/3.

[4] The scholarly track was organized jointly by the IIRF, the Initiative for the Study of Freedom of Religion or Belief (ISFORB) at the Evangelische Theologische Faculteit, and the Study Group on Religious Freedom, Persecution and Mission of the International Association for Mission Studies.

different continents and has a strong background as a practitioner as well, having worked for World Vision in Asia. She is an affiliated researcher at the Evangelische Theologische Faculteit. Having grown up in a multi-cultural and multi-religious context, Peirong is passionate about how Christian values can positively influence society. We appreciate her work in editing this important issue of the *IJRF*.

Yours for religious freedom,
Prof Dr Christof Sauer and Prof Dr Dr Thomas Schirrmacher, editors,
and Prof Dr Janet Epp Buckingham, managing editor

Introducing this issue

This issue presents some of the papers originally delivered in the scholarly tracks of the conferences referenced above, as well as other papers related to the issue of gender and persecution. Some of the papers are more recent than the 2016 date of this issue, which is being published in 2020 because the journal was dormant for several years.

The first opinion paper is by Emma Dipper, the founding director of the Gender and Religious Freedom Network. She traces the network's journey and provides more detail on how the topic of gender and religious freedom came to gain prominence.

In the second opinion paper, Olivia Jackson investigates how existing laws and public policies unwittingly discriminate against Christian women and the greater impact this could have on the church under pressure for its faith.

Amongst the peer-reviewed studies, Samuel Okanlawon provides a biblical exegesis of Galatians 3:28, arguing for the equality of men and women in Christ. This status of equality should inspire efforts to change the existing subjugation of women in society. Such action is crucial to the church's resilience and witness in the face of persecution.

Dennis Petri's paper introduces a methodological framework that can be used to determine the specificity of the vulnerability of females belonging to religious minority groups. Petri applies the framework to four case studies in which women suffered gender-specific pressures.

Becca Symes analyses the United Nations' responses to gendered religious persecution, based on a quantitative content analysis of UN documents and a series of interviews with experts. The findings suggest that the UN is inconsistent in its recognition of the intersectional vulnerability of gender and religious persecution. Significantly, various international declarations issued by UN Women have gradually stopped mentioning this intersection.

Saumya Uma examines the intersections between freedom of religion and women's equality rights in South Asia, reflecting on specific incidents and examples drawn from countries in the region. Uma concludes by highlighting the potential for a collaborative project between religious actors and women's rights advocates.

Rachel (a pseudonym) focuses on the resilience of religious minorities. She describes one particular approach, known as Strength2Stand, which has been used to increase the resilience of women belonging to Christian minorities. This self-help approach has been implemented in countries like Afghanistan, Pakistan and South Sudan.

Finally, Jayakumar Ramachandran discusses discrimination against women in India. He differentiates between discrimination in general and the experience of discrimination caused by one's Christian faith. Ramachandran analyses causes of this persecution and suggests solutions for the local church and Christians more broadly.

We have included an interesting variety of book reviews, some of which focus on gender and religious freedom issues. The Noteworthy section and the book reviews date to 2016.

We hope that you will find this issue as informative and compelling as we did when editing it.

Yours Sincerely,
Dr Peirong Lin
Guest editor

Publishers: Want to advertise a book?
Want your book listed under "Books Received"?
Reviewers: Want to review a book?
bookreviews@iirf.eu

Heiner Bielefeldt

Freedom of Religion or Belief:

Thematic Reports of the UN Special Rapporteur 2010 – 2016

Religious Freedom Series 3

VKW

Thomas Schirrmacher (Ed.)

The journey to a Gender and Religious Freedom Network

Emma Dipper[1]

Abstract
In the early 2000s, Release International and Open Doors realized that the persecution experienced by women was different than that experienced by men. This article details the development of the Gender and Religious Freedom Network, including conferences in Marcham UK, Leuven Belgium and Abuja Nigeria.

Keywords Women and religious freedom, gender and religious freedom, intersectionality.

How did we start talking about gender and persecution? It began with women. Multiple organizations and ministries were recognizing that the experience of Christian women facing persecution was very different from that of men. However, often the evidence was presented through a masculine lens that was neglecting the pressure points and cultural nuances that women faced.

At Release International, a UK sister entity to the Voice of the Martyrs organization founded by Richard Wurmbrand, a director came back from visiting India full of regret. He explained that a woman had shared deeply distressing stories of violence related to her Christian faith, but he felt it would have been culturally inappropriate to ask deeper questions, nor was he able offer her comfort through touch as she grew visibly distressed by recounting such trauma. For he was a man and she was a woman.

This event, along with those experienced by other male colleagues, led to the creation of a new department within Release International called Release Women, and I became its programme leader in 2009. The purpose was to develop specifically designed international projects focussed on women, so as to build their resilience to persecution, and to engage more strategically with women in the UK to fund these projects. There was no start-up funding and at the beginning, I was encouraged to work with a cost-neutral budget. Interestingly, this fact reflects a re-

---

[1] Emma Dipper is the founding director of Gender and Religious Freedom (www.genderandreligiousfreedom.org). She is based at All Nations Christian College, UK and is a lecturer in the theology of persecution, suffering mission and risk. She co-chairs the Gender and Religious Freedom Taskforce within the Religious Liberty Partnership and chairs the Gender and FoRB working group for the UK FoRB (freedom of religion and belief) Forum, where stakeholders and civil society groups hold the UK government accountable on FoRB issues. The article uses British English. Article submitted: 16 September 2020; accepted: 5 October 2020. Email: emma_dipper@yahoo.co.uk.

CHRISTIANS	Women	Men	Men ◄ ► Women
Weekly attendance	53%	46%	+7
Daily prayer	61%	51%	+10
Importance of Religion	68%	61%	+7
Belief in heaven	91%	89%	+2
Belief in hell	78%	76%	+1
Belief in angels	88%	84%	+3

MUSLIMS	Women	Men	Men ◄ ► Women
Weekly attendance	42%	70%	+7
Daily prayer	72%	71%	+2
Importance of Religion	76%	76%	0
Belief in heaven	94%	93%	0
Belief in hell	88%	88%	0
Belief in angels	86%	85%	+1

Table 1: Among Christians, woman are more religious than men on all measures; gender gaps among Muslims are less consistent. Average percentage-point difference between men and women on measures of religious practice, commitment and belief.

peated gender gap in funding of so-called 'women's ministry' projects, where most of the work is done by unpaid members of a larger team composed of voluntary and part-time staff. As the Rise in Strength gathering of 60 women leaders in June 2019, supported by the Lausanne Movement and the World Evangelical Alliance, stated, the top challenge for Christian women leaders is "the ability to raise the funds for the work which we feel called to."[2]

In the early years, the focus remained strictly on women. A similar development occurred within other organizations such as Open Doors. This was a sensible approach, supported by evidence from the Pew Research Forum (2016) that women had a greater affiliation with religion globally and that Christian women are more active in worship and church than men. As the projects grew with Release Women, the magnitude of the mission before us was overwhelming.

It was time for us to bring academics, practitioners and those experiencing persecution first-hand together, to collaborate and coordinate what we were doing and to be generous in sharing our learning and growth in this area.

---

[2] For more detail, see the Rise in Strength website, www.riseinstrength.net.

In 2016, in the village of Marcham just outside Oxford, UK, a group of 28 people gathered to discuss women and persecution. The event was scheduled immediately in advance of a Religious Liberty Partnership meeting that would become known as the Marcham Conference. Release International and the International Institute for Religious Freedom (IIRF), through the Evangelical Alliance in Denmark, helped to secure funding for what has become a movement and a network with an expanding global reach.

Throughout the three days, evidence was presented, and conversations were shared that resulted in the production of a "Message to the Global Church on the Double Vulnerability of Women due to Gender and Religion" (Marcham Message 2017). In that message, we declared:

> We grieve that:
> Women in such communities often face multiple forms of discrimination and violence, including restrictions on freedom of dress and movement, employment and legal discrimination, false charges, reprisals for conversion, sexual harassment, forced marriage, kidnapping, rape and other forms of sexual violence, including human trafficking.
> Women face violence within their homes, families and churches. This can include neglect, and verbal, physical, emotional, psychological, sexual and spiritual abuse. Such violence:
> - can also be experienced by wives of Christian leaders; many stories remain untold.
> - is a symptom of deeper issues, often driven by cultural and societal norms. Concerns include poor education, lack of teaching within the Church, lack of legal rights, lack of support services, and impunity for perpetrators.

The content of this letter was consistent with the messages shared by others working in this area across the globe. Three key aspects have emerged which have influenced further dialogues, research and consultations that occurred in Leuven, Belgium (2018) and Abuja, Nigeria (2019).

First, we needed to hear and understand more about the specific issues faced by men as well, along with more in-depth evidence concerning women. This information began to emerge in 2018 with the first of three exceptional reports from the World Watch Research Unit on 'Gender-Specific Religious Persecution' (Fisher and Miller 2018, 2019; Fisher, Miller and Mayer 2020). Second, we began to see that the pressure points for women facing persecution were invisible, complex and violent but that under-reporting was blinding the global church to this issue (Fisher and Miller 2018). Third, stark evidence continues to support our claim in the Marcham Letter that the church is complicit with those who violate women by offering impunity, making these actions low-risk to their perpetrators. The violations are overlooked due to existing societal and cultural norms that effectively dominate and silence the church (Fisher, Miller and Mayer 2020:22).

When women suffer as a result of their faith, the pain is not typically limited to a single act of violence or abuse. As women are persecuted through acts of gender-based violence and inequitable treatment, the effects break down the family unit, violate the perceived purity that their male relatives endorse and 'own,' and therefore shatter the Christian community. This is a highly effective strategy frequently applied by those who want to crush Christian minorities in their midst.

The profound trauma that these women face has been described as leaving them in a 'living death' (Fisher, Miller and Mayer 2020:16). Dolan (2011:128) highlights the effect on men being that "contrary to hegemonic models, they are unable to protect [and this] further breaks down the sense of self." Overlaying this problem are the under-reported acts of sexual violence towards men and forced participation in these atrocities, which could also impose their own version of 'living death' (or perhaps hidden death).

In terms of influence, how does a drop become a stream, then a river and finally a flood? In April 2018, a *kairos* moment occurred and both a philosophical and a practical change was initiated, as our focus on women and persecution shifted to *gender and religious freedom*. I was asked to deliver a presentation at a Religious Liberty Partnership (RLP) conference in Washington on women and persecution. By then, an effective and active steering group on the topic had been created with Helene Fisher and Elizabeth Miller from Open Doors, Christof Sauer of the IIRF, and myself. I requested that we do a joint presentation so that we could share the findings on 'Gender-Specific Religious Persecution' from World Watch Research (Fisher and Miller 2018). The RLP targets key decision makers and leaders in this field; thus our audience was 80% male. As we prepared, we had a sense that we were embarking on more than a presentation, and that God seemed to be moving us into a space or time of which we understood little. We made sure to begin with the specific persecution that men suffer. We progressed to present on women in the same way; by then, this mostly male gathering was fully engaged in the greater and tragic complexities of gender-specific persecution.

The next day, the RLP was invited to meet with members of the U.S. Senate on Capitol Hill. Before we left Washington, significant alliances and relationships were formed that continue to aid our work, and Gender and Religious Freedom had become task force of the RLP.

Since then, we have worked closely with the World Evangelical Alliance in presenting on this subject at the UN Commission for the Status of Women in 2018 and 2019. More government committees for freedom of religion and belief (FoRB) have engaged with this topic, such as those in the Netherlands, UK, USA and Canada. Our recommendations were included in the Bishop of Truro's report on the persecution of Christians (UK), and we continue to have a very good relationship with the Foreign and Commonwealth Office (now known as the Foreign, Commonwealth and Development Office), having just been requested to lead a Gender and FoRB Working Group for the UK FoRB Forum. Gender issues are being mainstreamed in several ministries and organizations, yet some remain silent on the issue.

In today's context, gender is a complicated and complex subject, one that is being redefined and even reimagined. As people of faith, we need to discuss and wrestle with this situation. But if we have learnt anything about gender and persecution, it is that we need to sit with those who are in deep pain because of how they are defined and treated, and not marginalize them as we have done with women for millennia.

Our network, Gender and Religious Freedom are increasingly welcomed in spaces where we can debate and listen to others with contrary views, always giving and in the hope of receiving respect and dignity.

I have heard time and time again that women are the 'emotional ones' and that men 'do the facts and don't engage in emotion.' I have further heard that women are less effective leaders because of their lack of objectivity. None of these statements are true.

As people of faith, we have a Creator who feels deeply about the issues raised here and in all the articles in this journal. If we deny our own emotions, we deny that part of the Creator's image that we all bear. Emotion is often minimized or disallowed in the field of FoRB. We deliver the facts, we write statements of 'deep concern,' or we craft an advocacy policy and organize an event with people of power and influence. But when do we give ourselves and each other time to feel and express the pain, injustice and anger that we *should* be feeling because women and men of religious minorities are facing more violence and discrimination than ever before?

A Nigerian female pastor shared with a small steering group for Release Women in 2016 just before the Marcham Conference. She ended by saying, "Weep until heaven has no choice but to open the doors. It's time for a divine strategy! Then stop weeping and get on."

1. Vision and aims of the Gender and Religious Freedom Network
1.1 Our vision
- ➢ We aim to unlock and expand the resilience of Christian women and men experiencing persecution for their faith.
- ➢ We are women and men who recognise the complex and hidden nature of gender-specific persecution of Christian women and girls, alongside the severe and focused nature of religious persecution of men and boys.

- We are a forum committed to hearing the authentic voice of women, whilst not negating the known ways in which men suffer for their faith.
- We are committed to collaborative, evidence-based and multidisciplinary approaches.

1.2 Our aims

- *To create space* both online and in person to share relevant research, reports and broader communications on the subject of gender and religious persecution. This includes updating the website, online webinars and training and consultations.
- *To be an accessible network* that ensures expertise aiming for change at the grassroots and through policy and practices at its highest level. This will be done through connections in this forum and with other networks that intersect in wider areas of influence. Also, in joining Freedom of Religions or Belief (FoRB) forums and working groups allied to government departments and international bodies.
- *To work for the good of all in our field of influence* we actively avoid competition between organisations or individuals but promote the achievements of all whilst contributing with robust and respectful debate and discussion where appropriate.
- *To be intentionally intergenerational*, reaching out to those beginning their career in the area of FoRB or ministries in gender and religious persecution. We create interactions that enhance mentoring between those with expertise or first-hand experience and those who are growing and developing in this field. However, everyone is learning.
- *To be create equity of voice*. This means that we aim for sharing platforms of influence without hierarchy or primacy ensuring that our communication allows for women or men, old or young, any nation, tribe or tongue to be represented and valued.
- *As a forum, we are Christian and we believe in freedom of religion* for all faiths or none. This means we aim to work and network across all faith-based, civil and secular organisations and will advocate for all but are unashamedly part of the global Church and seek to build its resilience as our vision states.

References

Dolan, Chris. 2011. 'Militarized, Religious and Neo-Colonial. The Triple Blind Confronting Men in Contemporary Uganda', in Cornwall, Andrea, Jerker Edstrom and Alan Greig, *Men and Development: Political Masculinities*. London and New York: Zed Books, pp. 127-138.

Fisher, Helene and Elizabeth Miller. 2018. *Gendered Persecution: World Watch List 2018 Analysis and Implications*. Open Doors International. Available at: https://bit.ly/33BxZGY.

Fisher, Helene and Elizabeth Miller. 2019. *WWL 2019 Analysis of Gender Specific Persecution: Analysis and Implications*. Open Doors Analytics. Available at: https://bit.ly/34tqscM.

Fisher, Helene and Elizabeth Miller. 2020. *World Watch Research 2020: Gender-Specific Religious Persecution: Analysis and Implications*. Santa Ana, CA: World Watch Research.

Marcham Message 2017. 'Message to the Global Church on the Double Vulnerability of Women due to Gender and Religion.' in Johnson, Thomas, Thomas Schirrmacher and Christof Sauer (eds.), *Global Statements on Freedom of Religion or Belief*. Bonn: Culture and Science Publishing, pp.115-171. Available at: https://bit.ly/3d97LPk.

Mounstephen, Philip. 2019. *Bishop of Truro's Independent Review for the Foreign Secretary of FCO Support for Persecuted Christians. Final Report and Recommendations*. Available at: https://bit.ly/3d5vnnR.

Pew Research Center. 2016. *The Gender Gap in Religion Around the World*. Available at: https://pewrsr.ch/3nsaKao.

FIGHTING

OVER

GOD

A Legal and Political History of Religious Freedom in Canada

JANET EPP BUCKINGHAM

The restricted legal status of women
An inconvenience for Christian women or a vulnerability for the church?
Olivia Jackson[1]

Abstract

In many countries, minority religious women face double persecution. First, they face laws that are discriminatory against women. Second, laws discriminate against religious minorities. This is so in both the public and private realms. The article explores the intersectionality that minority religious women face, particularly in Middle Eastern societies.

Keywords Intersectionality, discrimination against women, direct discrimination, indirect discrimination.

1. Introduction

The intersection between discrimination against women with religious persecution creates an effective, and sometimes legally sanctioned, means of indirectly attacking minority religions, even where religious freedom exists under law. International bodies such as the United Nations have cautioned that "laws and public policies developed to protect culture and religion that threaten the universally established standards on the rights of women" increase the vulnerability of women who do not conform to the mainstream to "discrimination, violence and criminalization" (Human Rights Council 2015:7).

Scarce concrete evidence exists concerning the intentional use of gender-restrictive laws to target Christians for persecution; most verifiable records of discrimination or violence against women do not disaggregate along religious lines. Where there is no recourse to justice, establishing intersectionality is usually impossible. Given the lack of statistical information and verifiable reports, plus the understandable silence of women themselves, this paper highlights how restrictive legal frameworks can doubly discriminate against Christians, intentionally or not, and the impact this has on the persecuted Church.

---

[1] Olivia Jackson (LLM, University of London) has worked as a human rights consultant specializing in the strategic use of violence against women, including religious persecution. This article is based on the paper she presented at the Women Under Pressure for Their Faith conference, Leuven, Belgium, 2017. The article uses British spelling. Article received: 31 July 2020; accepted: 10 September 2020. E-mail: oliviajackson@mac.com.

2. Ways in which laws fail women

Laws discriminate in two primary ways: directly and indirectly. Direct discrimination is a clear disadvantaging of one group in relation to another. Indirect discrimination appears to affect everyone equally but has a disproportionate impact on one group; for example, the 2016 ban on religiously affiliated or full-body beachwear in parts of France appears to affect everyone, but actually affects only Muslim women. Likewise, Myanmar's Health Care for Population Control Act (2015), allowing authorities to 'organise' birth spacing, applies to all groups but is most likely to target women from marginalized religious groups.

Legal frameworks also fail vulnerable groups through inadequate or outright lack of legal provision or protection – for example, if no law exists against domestic violence. Where protective laws do exist, state actors may fail to enforce them or show bias in the administration of justice, such as when police discourage women from reporting assaults or refuse to take reports (there is anecdotal evidence of this pattern in Pakistan, with Christian families allegedly being told that complaints will incite inter-communal violence); the differential treatment of women or Christians by judges; or the failure to ensure universal access to the law, which often hits the poor and minorities hardest.

3. The public–private dichotomy
3.1 The public sphere

Many nations discriminate against women to different degrees in different areas of society. Mayer (1984) wrote that women in Middle Eastern societies have sometimes had public rights pre-dating those of women in the West, such as the right to stand for office (consider such public figures as Benazir Bhutto of Pakistan and Sheikh Hasina Wajed of Bangladesh), but their private-sphere rights are more restrictive. Despite this observation, limitations of public-sphere rights clearly exist.

UNICEF (2011) listed 14 Middle East and North African countries[2] where a woman's testimony in certain court cases was worth half that of a man.[3] Blasphemy laws thus offer an easy way to attack the Church, as Christian women have little defence against a male accuser. Although most accusations of blasphemy in Pa-

---

[2] Bahrain (in Sharia courts); Egypt (in family courts); Iran (in most cases); Iraq (in some cases); Jordan (in Sharia courts); Kuwait (in family courts); Libya (in some cases); Morocco (in family courts); Palestine (in cases related to marriage, divorce and child custody); Qatar (in family law matters); Saudi Arabia; Syria (in Sharia courts); United Arab Emirates (in some civil matters); Yemen (not allowed to testify at all in cases of adultery and retribution).

[3] Pakistan's Law of Evidence (1984) also considers the evidence of a woman as worth half that of a man and the evidence of a non-Muslim worth half that of a Muslim in certain cases, leaving non-Muslim women effectively without defence.

kistan, for instance, are levelled at Sunnis, a disproportionately high number are aimed at minorities. The National Commission on Justice and Peace has recorded instances of Christian women converting to Islam to escape punishment for 'blasphemy' (Haider 2011:113–15).

In Iran, the age of criminal responsibility is 15 for boys but 9 for girls. Article 102 of the Penal Code states, "For the purpose of stoning, the man shall be buried into a pit up to his waist and the woman up to her breast" to reduce any chance of escape.

Restrictions on women's employment cause impoverished Christian families to lose vital income. Richards and Haglund (2015) correlated women's increased economic empowerment with government enforcement of laws condemning violence against women. Other evidence (e.g. UNICEF 2004:19) shows that the rate of maternal and infant mortality rises when women are denied education.

Even when discrimination affects all women, the effect is greater on pressured groups: Christian Solidarity Worldwide (n.d.) has reported lower levels of education amongst Christian and Hindu Pakistani women than amongst the general population, and most of those not in school are girls (Human Rights Watch 2018).

3.2 The private sphere

Women in these societies face more severe restrictions in the private sphere. These limitations spring from beliefs about gender roles, lack of agency, women's honour affecting the entire family, the dangers of female sexuality and the perception of women as the property of male family members. Quraishi (1997:298–99) wrote, "This attitude lends itself easily to manipulation and the development of a tribal attitude where women's bodies become tools for revenge by men against men." Countries such as Afghanistan[4] that give women equal rights under their constitution devolve private-sphere law to parallel justice systems, including tribal and Sharia courts.

Saudi Arabia and Iran are amongst the countries that place restrictions on women's everyday life in the name of protecting them. These strictures are not overtly violent, but subjection to daily indignities severely impairs both women's ability to participate in society and their quality of life. The requirement to have a male chaperone, for instance, constrains women's freedom to leave an abusive situation or be admitted to a hospital without a husband's permission. As a minority group,

---

[4] Article 22 of the Constitution of Afghanistan states, "Any kind of discrimination and distinction between citizens of Afghanistan shall be forbidden. The citizens of Afghanistan, man and woman, have equal rights and duties before the law." However, the Shia Personal Status Law of 2009, Article 133, declares as follows: "(1) The household's supervision is the right of the husband, unless based on the husband's mental deficiency, and by order of the court, it is given to the wife. (2) A wife can leave the house for legal purposes to the extent that local custom allows."

Christian women can thus become more isolated and less visible to the general population, entrenching their 'otherness.'

Indirect discrimination is apparent when countries make no provision for differential healthcare for men and women, or when they under-prioritize services used only by women, such as ignoring women's reproductive health needs. Substantive equality does sometimes require the law to acknowledge differences.

The ways in which domestic life legally discriminates against women read like a catalogue of oppression across a range of countries:
- Lower age of marriage for girls than for boys
- Dowry entitlement
- Right to manage property
- Children's citizenship can be inherited only from the father
- The husband is the legal head of the household and his wife must obey him
- Male polygamy and temporary marriage
- Prescribed number of children, and/or the spacing between them
- Difference between the two genders in the ability to divorce or grounds for divorce
- Post-divorce child custody and property settlement
- Inequalities in succession and inheritance rights
- Barriers to employment, such as required spousal consent and lack of maternity policies
- Entitlement to state benefits
- Discrimination with regard to inter-faith marriages[5]
- Status of widows

In addition, the most obviously dangerous examples of laws or lack of protections include the non-criminalization of domestic violence and marital rape, as well as reduced legal liability for honour-based violence, including homicide, especially if the victim's family forgives the perpetrator(s). As most honour killings are committed by family members, this provision effectively guarantees impunity. For the female Christian convert in a family of non-believers, this can make practising her faith unbearable or even deadly. As of 2018, 24 percent of countries lacked laws against domestic violence, 51 percent had no laws against domestic economic violence and 37 percent of countries lacked specific laws against domestic sexual violence. Overall nearly 1.1 billion women lack legal protection against sexual violence by an intimate partner or family member (Tavares and Wodon 2018).

---

[5] Laws to this effect exist in Myanmar, Bangladesh and Egypt. For example, if a Muslim woman cannot marry a Christian man but a Christian woman can marry a Muslim man, this provision ensures that legal heads of inter-faith households and any children of such marriages will always be Muslims. If conversion to Christianity is not recognized, female converts still cannot marry as they remain legally Muslim.

Laws criminalizing extra-marital sex often appear gender-neutral, but women's subordinate position in most cultures means that they are far more vulnerable to violation, accusations and harsh sentencing for this crime, particularly where the legal line between consensual and coerced sex is blurred. A comparison of the numbers and sentences of women and men imprisoned and/or executed for adultery, fornication and prostitution shows vast gender-based disparities.[6]

Violence against women can thus be perpetrated with impunity; if the woman cannot prove rape, such as by providing witnesses, she may be prosecuted for engaging in extra-marital sex.[7] At least nine countries exonerate a rapist if he marries his victim.[8] Marriage often confers less shame on the victim's family, providing an incentive to allow it. Christian families, whose daughter, as a result of having been raped, is far less likely to find a Christian husband, may come under additional community pressure to agree. Such laws show the extent to which justice for women is attached to their community standards, rather than to an unbiased legal system.

Even without prosecution, the stigma of accusation or of surviving rape often leads to lifelong ostracism, even from the Christian community, thereby adding to existing trauma. Women are effectively removed from the community in this way. When the Church engages in a prevailing culture of gender disparity, violence and shame, it sabotages itself and does the work of its persecutors itself.

4. Conclusion

Discriminatory laws fundamentally undermine whole nations and the Church within them. A woman who is not free from violence, not free to move around, and not free to be educated or to earn a living is less able to be a contributing member of

---

[6] UN CEDAW Committee, quoted in Raday (2012: 6) regarding Pakistan: "High percentage of women and girls in jails awaiting trials for adultery-related hudood offences and at the imposition, by parallel judicial systems, of sentences like whipping, amputation and stoning amounting to torture or cruel, inhuman or degrading treatment"; regarding Yemen: "The majority of women in prison have been sentenced for prostitution, adultery, alcoholism, unlawful or indecent behaviour, in a private or public setting, as well as for violating restrictions of movement imposed by family traditions and Yemeni laws; such sentences are applied in a discriminatory way against women."

[7] In 2008, 13-year-old gang-rape victim Aisha Ibrahim Duhulow was publicly stoned to death in Somalia for adultery because she could not provide witnesses. Her complaint was viewed as a confession and her attackers were not arrested.

[8] "Bahrain, Iraq, Jordan, Kuwait, Lebanon, Palestine, Philippines, Tajikistan and Tunisia. It also appears possible in Greece and Russia, Serbia and Thailand, in circumstances where the couple are in a sexual relationship and under the law the girl is otherwise deemed too young to consent to sexual intercourse. A perpetrator can be exempt from punishment by reaching a 'settlement,' financial or otherwise, with the victim or the victim's family in at least 12 (out of 82) jurisdictions. These are Belgium, Croatia, Iraq, Jordan, Kazakhstan, Lebanon, Palestine, Nigeria, Romania, Russia, Singapore and Thailand" (Hassan 2017). As of this writing, Jordan and Tunisia have repealed these laws, and Lebanon has repealed with some loopholes remaining.

her family or society. These laws, or the lack of protections against discrimination, undermine the value of women's lives.

Legal systems which enshrine gender inequality generally also enshrine other inequalities, such as restrictions on religious freedom. Treating men and women as equals is foundational to treating all groups justly. The intersection of gender and religious persecution creates a double discrimination, even before gender is used as a basis for indirect persecution. It is in the Church's interest to fight discrimination against all women, not only for the benefit of Christian women and to strengthen the Church, but also because restrictive and inadequate laws condone violence against women and damage whole societies. These laws are not merely an inconvenience; they are lethal.

References

Christian Solidarity Worldwide. n.d.. *Pakistan: Christian Solidarity Worldwide*. Available at: http://www.csw.org.uk/our_work_profile_pakistan.htm.

Haider, Yasmin. 2011. 'Non-Muslim Women in Pakistan: Minority Within Minority', in Ahlstrand, Kajsa and Göran Gunner (eds.) *Non-Muslims in Muslim Majority Societies: With Focus on the Middle East and Pakistan*, Cambridge: The Lutterworth Press, pp.108-116.

Hassan, Yasmeen. 2017. *The World's Shame: The Global Rape Epidemic* (ebook). Equality Now. Available at: https://bit.ly/30JN7QO.

Human Rights Council. 2015. *Report of the Working Group on the Issue of Discrimination against Women in Law and in Practice (A/HRC/29/40)*. United Nations Office of the High Commissioner for Human Rights.

Human Rights Watch. 2015. 'Burma: Reject Discriminatory Population Bill'. Available at: https://www.hrw.org/news/2015/05/16/burma-reject-discriminatory-population-bill.

Human Rights Watch. 2018. 'Shall I Feed My Daughter, or Educate Her? Barriers to Girls' Education in Pakistan'. Available at: https://www.hrw.org/report/2018/11/12/shall-i-feed-my-daughter-or-educate-her/barriers-girls-education-pakistan.

Mayer, Ann Elizabeth. 1984. 'Law and Women in the Middle East', *Cultural Survival Quarterly Magazine* 8(2). Available at: https://bit.ly/37Zq0pK.

Quraishi, Asifa. 1997. 'Her Honor: An Islamic Critique of the Rape Laws of Pakistan from a Woman-Sensitive Perspective', *Michigan Journal of International Law* 18(2), pp. 287-320.

Raday, Frances. 2012. *Background Information on the Statement by the United Nations Working Group on Discrimination against Women in Law and in Practice*. United Nations Office of the High Commissioner for Human Rights, [online]. Available by link at: https://bit.ly/3nxUHrq.

Richards, David and Haglund, Jillienne. 2015. How Laws Around the World Do and Do Not Protect Women from Violence. *Washington Post*. Available at: https://wapo.st/3jJehPo.

Tavares, Paula and Wodon, Quentin. 2018. *Ending Violence Against Women and Girls: Global and Regional Trends in Women's Legal Protection Against Domestic and Sexual Harassment.* World Bank, [online]. Available at: https://bit.ly/3lj8Gj8.

UNICEF. 2004. *State of the World's Children Report.* Available at: https://www.unicef.org/sowc04/files/SOWC_O4_eng.pdf.

UNICEF. 2011. *Regional Overview for the Middle East and North Africa Region.* Available at: https://www.unicef.org/gender/files/REGIONAL-Gender-Eqaulity-Profile-2011.pdf.

Christians under Pressure: Studies in Discrimination and Persecution 2

Kay Bascom

Overcomers

*God's deliverance through the
Ethiopian Revolution as witnessed
primarily by the Kale Heywet Church community*

VKW

"There is neither male nor female"
Theological reflection on Galatians 3:28 as a faith-based response to gender-specific persecution

Samuel Oluwatosin Okanlawon[1]

Abstract

This paper considers the paradigmatic Pauline assertion in Galatians 3:28, "There is neither male nor female," as a faith-based approach to counter gender-specific persecution of women and girls. Drawing on Vander Watt's hermeneutic theory of contextual relevance, I propose that Paul elevates the female gender to the level of equality with males, on the basis of having been saved by Christ. Therefore, gender distinctions between males and females in their essence and nature, which cause females to be restricted in the expression of personhood within the Christian community, are removed. Females should not be disempowered within or outside the church community in any form on the basis of their sex.

Keywords Gender-specific persecution, Pauline theology, women, church, Galatians 3:28.

1. Introduction

Persecution generally involves the unfair treatment and subjugation of another person. It often includes physical brutality and is widely viewed as a serious violation of human rights. It is also the cumulative effect of numerous harms that affect a person's subjective psychological make-up (Kelly 1993:645). Therefore, any actions and rules that demean and subjugate any person can be classified as persecution.

Gender-specific persecution (GsP)[2] can affect men or women, but women are disproportionately affected because of the unequal power relationships and structures within families, communities and countries. These inequalities can spill over into church settings, causing women to have limited decision-making power and

---

[1] Samuel Oluwatosin Okanlawon, PhD is a Senior Lecturer in Christian Theology, Department of Religious Studies, University of Ibadan, Ibadan, Oyo State, Nigeria. His research activity includes ensuring that female members of the ecclesiastical community are given more space to express their spiritual giftedness alongside their male counterparts and counter the marginalization of women and girls. This article uses British English. Article submitted: 11 April 2019; accepted: 12 May 2020. Email: samtoscares@yahoo.com; so.okanlawon@ui.edu.ng.

[2] In the context of this paper, gender-specific persecution relates to persecution resulting from a person's sex, most commonly persecution of women because they are women.

to be under-represented in the church's leadership structure. Gender distinction, rather than gender distinctiveness, leads to GsP. Actions and attitudes that demean or subjugate women in the church context and which can be considered gender-specific include, but are not limited to, excluding women from some ecclesiastical offices (Kasomo 2010:129), theologies of women's silence, submission and sacrificial suffering (Fisher, Miller and Mayer 2020:35-36), and biblical interpretations that describe women as sinners, manipulators and temptresses. These actions are not found in every church congregation, and especially not in social contexts characterized by true democratic governance.

Previous studies of GsP have largely concerned national and international asylum laws and guidelines related to the topic (Kelly 1993; Hagglund 2015; LaViolette 2008; Chertoff 2017; Harris 2009), female refugee situations (Marshall and Barret, 2018; Crawley 2001; Haines 2003; Kirk 2010; United Nations High Commissioner on Refugees [UNHCR] 2008; Ankerbrand 2002; Anker 2001), feminist and gender-equality settings (Freedman 2015; Greatbach 1989), and the situation within the Christian community (Gilbert 2018; Moore 2015). Despite the contributions of these studies, this discourse needs to be further emphasized within the Christian community, especially as it relates to the non-physical persecution of women and girls.

Therefore, this paper examines the Pauline paradigm, "There is neither male nor female," in Galatians 3:28 as a faith-based approach to counter GsP of women and girls within the Christian community, from the perspective of a Christian based in Africa. I draw on J. G. Vander Watt's hermeneutic theory of contextual relevance, which emphasizes the similar and dissimilar elements between the world of the biblical text and that of the interpreter in the act of biblical interpretation. The relevant data come from the biblical text and analyses thereof, along with published materials on GsP. The focus is on derogatory attitudes towards women in the church that demean and subjugate them despite their status as God's creatures.

2. Gender-based persecution of women

Gender-based persecutions of women are connected by the common threat of gendered relations and power relations that ascribe particular roles and behaviours to women. They include the use of sexual violence as a means of power and control over women, forced marriage, targeted seduction and militia conscription (Fisher and Miller 2019:2). Also, they are based on a dysfunctional and hegemonic interpretation of the female gender, rooted in socio-cultural constructs (Fisher and Miller 2019:5) that question women's capacity to be human and declare that men must be in control. Sultana (2012:3-5) refers to this pattern as the "institutionalization of male dominance over women" and notes that it unavoidably upholds women's dependence on men.

Most practices relating to the gender-based persecution of women are grounded more in attitudes than in specific actions. They often emanate from a religious and cultural ethos that has grown out of the misinterpretation of religious texts and the misappropriation of oral traditions embedded in a culture. In the church context, women are sometimes persecuted for having transgressed the supposedly traditional mores of Christianity. Some consider women to be a second-level creation of God and so inferior to men; thus, they conclude, women should be subservient to men even in carrying out ecclesiastical roles.

In the context of this paper and Galatians 3:28, the persecution of women is not physical in nature; rather, it takes a form that demeans and devalues beings who were created in God's image. This devaluation of women can cause great psychological trauma and self-perception as inferior. It consists of the unequal and unfair treatment of women and girls on the basis of their being female. It is an internalized, ecclesial persecution rather than an externalized, violent one. Some consequences of this form of persecution are the domestication of women, regulation and control of women's sexuality (Sultana 2012:4), prevention of women from exercising their full human rights, reduction of their participation in the full life of the ecclesial communities, low self-esteem, low self-confidence, and increased risk of depression and anxiety.

3. The context of Galatians 3:28

The passage being considered comes as the climax of a discussion concerning the relationship between law and faith in Christ that runs throughout Galatians 3. It furthers Paul's discourse on justification by faith or by observance of the law. Generally, Galatians was written as a protest against the corruption of Christ's gospel (Tenney 1989). Thus, Christian liberty is the central theme of Galatians.

The context of Galatians 3:28 concerns, first, the nature of justification or, more specifically, the condition of full membership in the Abrahamic covenant with its attendant blessings. Second, it discusses the social implications of being saved (Davis 1976; MacArthur 2010; Balge 1981). Paul's immediate aim in writing was to dissuade the Galatian believers from submitting to circumcision and from conforming to Jewish identity as an essential prerequisite for participating in God's new covenantal people.

The Judaizing heresy, whereby Jewish Christians were compelling the Gentile Christians to live by Jewish practices (1:6-7; 5:2-3, 12; 6:11-15), and circumcision in particular, had become prevalent in Galatia (Donovan 2016). The Judaizers were demanding Torah observance. At the time when Paul wrote this letter, there was a deep division between two cultures within the body of Christ: Jews and Gentiles. The Gentile was uncircumcised and was previously no child of Abraham. But in Christ, the barrier has now been broken (Ephesians 2:11-18). Therefore, no distinguishing qualities are important for entrance into or functioning within the church of Christ.

4. Interpreting Galatians 3:28

Galatians 3:28: οὐκ ἔνι Ἰουδαῖος οὐδὲ Ἕλλην, οὐκ ἔνι δοῦλος οὐδὲ ἐλεύθερος, οὐκ ἔνι ἄρσεν καὶ θῆλυ· πάντες γὰρ ὑμεῖς εἷς ἐστε ἐν Χριστῷ Ἰησοῦ.
There is neither Jew nor Gentile, neither slave nor free, nor is there male and female, for you are all one in Christ Jesus (NIV).

Fung (1988) states that Galatians 3:28 falls within Paul's exposition of the purpose of the law, that is, to be a slave-guardian on the path towards maturity and unrestricted enjoyment of sonship (cf. 3:24; 4:1-7). This verse is part of a paragraph that commences at vv. 26-27: "For you are all God's sons through faith in Christ Jesus. For so many of you as were baptized into Christ have put on Christ" (KJV). This is Paul's affirmation of the believers' status in Christ. He then mentions, in v. 28, a triple pair of distinctions, by ethnicity, social class and gender. The verse emphasizes the vertical consequence of salvation for the believer (i.e. our relationship to God). "There is no male or female" is followed by "You are all one in Christ Jesus."

Grobler (2011) notes that Galatians 3:28 is made up of three negated couplets as well as an explanatory clause. Two of these couplets are positioned within the recipe that there is no "there is neither" X *oude* Y (X nor Y), but the third couplet contains a slight change: "there is neither male 'καὶ' (and) female." A different combination is apparently used here to connect two contrasting nouns. Degner (2001) says that the reason is not totally clear, but that when "male" (ἔνι ἄρσεν) occurs with "female" (θῆλυ·), the couplet is almost always καὶ. Hove (1999) argues that the variation, in conjunction with the third pair, is an intentional reference to Genesis, where God created humanity as "male and female" prior to the Fall, and it was very good (Genesis 1:27, 31).

Paul's declaration that there is "neither male and female" stands in marked contrast to commonly accepted patterns of privilege and prejudice in the ancient world. Women were considered inferior within both Jewish and Greek culture. Hellenistic men regularly thanked God for allowing them to be born as human beings and not as beasts, as Greeks and not as barbarians, as citizens and not as slaves, as men and not as women. Jewish men commonly recited a prayer each morning which stated, "I thank thee, God, that thou hast not made me a slave or a woman or a Gentile dog" (Esler 2014).

Hence, Paul is emphasizing in Galatians 3:26-28 that men and women enjoy a new, equal and exalted status before God. Thus, the female gender has been raised from degradation and denigration. Earthly relationships are put in the perspective of salvation history. All persons in Christ have the same salvation status before God, though they do not necessarily have the same function. There are no ethnic, economic or gender distinctions. This was contrary to the cosmopolitanism being promoted by Paul's contemporaries (i.e. Greek philosophers) in the first century. Paul promoted the community of all human beings. His use of contrasts in this verse covers the full range of the most profound distinctions made within human society: racial or cultural, social or economic, sexual or gender-based (Witherington 2009). Paul does not intend these three divisions as comprehensive, but rather as illustrative. He is saying that, in Christ, all the barriers that divide one person from another are rendered null and void.

According to most Bible scholars, Paul's emphasis in this verse is not on abolishing gender differences, promulgating the Magna Carta of gender equality, or denying human categories generally (Botha 2000; Gundry-Volf 1997; Eisenbaum 2000; Witherington 2009). His concern is to show that neither being male nor being female is of any importance for being in Christ. As Gundry-Volf (1997) asserts, Paul has the "adiaphorization (this word comes from the Greek adiaphora for indifferent matters) of sex difference" in mind. This means that being male or female does not bring any advantage or disadvantage. Tolmie (2014) concurs that there is a deconstruction of the male hegemonic sentimentalities that pervaded the religio-socio-cultural contexts of Paul's time. The apostle re-prioritises ethnic, socio-economic and gender identities by subordinating them to "being in Christ." Modern sociologists term this process "recategorization" (Brawley 2014). Every other distinction, including gender distinction, is subordinated to the Christian identity, which becomes the superior identity.

Paul, in Galatians 3:28, elevates the female gender to equality with males on the basis of their salvation status in Christ, within a socio-religio-cultural context that had denigrated and degraded the female sex. Thus, gender distinctions between males and females, in their essence and nature, are removed and a complementary relationship between both sexes is established. This does not deny that the roles women and men play in the family, church or other communal contexts may be not different, dependent on the particular context. Paul envisages a social ideal of harmony and connection, where those factors in the society that create division, conflict, and persecution have been removed.

5. Theological reflection on Galatians 3:28 in relation to gender-specific persecution of women

One's theological viewpoint determines one's actions and reactions. Theology drives practice. The theological implication of this verse is that as the gospel has changed our vertical relationship (God to humans), it also changes our horizontal relationships (person to person). Paul's emphasis is on the relationship between ethics (Christian behaviour) and theology.

Paul's logic in Galatians 3:28 applies to ethnicity, class and gender. His theology calls for inclusiveness in ethnic, social and gender terms. With respect to gender, the arguments against women serving in positions of church leadership are much the same as the arguments presumably made by Paul's opponents to restrict leadership to Jewish believers only. He writes against the dominating gender construct of ethno-Jewish and Hellenistic-Roman society. It was tailored towards developing a radically new, Christian mindset within the existing cultural and religious context.

Paul's theology in Galatians 3:28 is not only soteriological but ecclesiological. As Fee (2000) asserts, it would be theologically disastrous to divorce ecclesiology from soteriology in this passage. Appealing to Galatians 2:11-14, Snodgrass (1986) contends that the phrase "male and female" in Galatians 3:28 has social implications, which lead to encouraging women to participate in ministry as they did in the New Testament. This is an indication of ecclesiastical equality. Paul's corporate Christology introduces within the Christian community a non-gendered valuation of persons belonging to that community. The old dualisms (Jew-Gentile, free-slave, male-female) are obliterated. Paul argues for a corporate identity that is geared towards social unity.

This teaching is not based on the current climate of the culture. It is not liberal, conservative or political; rather, it is the direct result of the gospel. It is a statement about our equal value in the eyes of God and about how we should learn to view one another. Since all Christians are in Christ, we are all one. The racial, social or gender identities that formerly divided the people have lost significance. God no longer sees human distinctions. Therefore, we must not prevent women from taking up leadership positions in the church. The calling to even the ministerial offices identified in Ephesians 4:11 is a *charisma*, a gift of the Spirit. If God has gifted a woman, who are we to resist?

There is no enumeration of gender-specific tasks in the New Testament (Romans 12:3-6). As 1 Corinthians 12 points out, the church is the body of Christ, so every member of the body – that is, each Christian – functions as they are equipped or graced. Moreover, redemption has made males and females of equal status. Thus, by implication, the dignity of both males and females is of equal importance and the church, as an institution, must endeavour to eliminate all situations that promote non-violent persecution and erode the dignity of persons God has elevated. The church must especially protect the dignity of women and girls because they are more vulnerable. We should not use the specific ecclesial contexts of 1 Timothy 2:11-15 and Titus 2:4-5 to override a generalized ecclesial context indicated in Galatians 3:28. Paul affirms the full equality of men and women in ministry in other passages as well (1 Corinthians 11:5; 12:12-20; Romans 12:4-5, 16; Colossians 3:15).

In the church, our nationality, status and sex remain. No one should be discriminated against or persecuted on the basis of that person's gender, race or economic status. God's act of creating humanity in Genesis 1:27 shows that God created gender as constitutive for the human condition. The distinction between male and female is essential for propagation of the human family, as introduced by God before the Fall (Genesis 3). Men and women function differently in the Christian community, but no one should be limited in operation on the basis of their gender.

6. Recommendations for action

The following recommendations for action arise from the foregoing analysis:
1. Christian theologians should continue to articulate a theology that encompasses violent and non-violent persecution, rather than addressing only the persecution that inflicts physical pain and injury, and to adapt this theology to present-day circumstances. This is a necessary part of the clamour for religious freedom.
2. Academic theology should emphasize the interconnectedness of both male and female roles within the ecclesial community through relevant topics in church history, biblical studies, practical theology and missiology.
3. Church leaders and theologians should provide a counter-cultural response, in relation to the subjugation of women in the church, through teachings and practices that elevate the personhood of Christian women and girls. This is crucial to the church's resiliency and witness in the midst of violent and non-violent persecution.
4. Christian women must be given the latitude to exercise their spiritual gifts along with men, including being placed in any hierarchy of church leadership as affirmed in Ephesians 4:11-16, to keep the body of Christ functioning appropriately. The walls of socio-cultural stereotypes must not be erected in the church, for they will become an instrument of gender persecution and will curtail religious freedom.

7. Conclusion

The radical shift towards inclusion of women at all levels of church leadership that began in the twentieth century must be sustained. This push is not just for gender equality but for gender equity and complementarity. Christian women should not be defined by sexuality and reproduction, but as veritable and equal partners in church life, in a variety of capacities as the Holy Spirit empowers. Both chauvinism and feminism are wrong; men and women should be allowed to fulfil their callings to minister to God's people and to care for creation in their own unique ways. An appropriate contextual interpretation and application of Galatians 3:28 prevent the text from being used as a theological trump card to promote discrimination, segregation and competition.

References

Anker, Deborah. 2001. 'Refugee status and violence against women in the 'domestic' sphere: The non-state actor question', *Georgetown Immigration Law Journal*, 15, pp. 391-402.

Ankenbrand, Birthe. 2002. 'Refugee women under German asylum law', *International Journal of Refugee Law*, 14(1), pp. 45-56.

Balge, R. 1981. 'An exegetical study of Galatians 3:28: "There is no male and female … in Christ Jesus"', [online]. Available at: https://bit.ly/3iFXafQ.

Botha, Pieter. 2000) 'Submission and violence: Exploring gender relations in the first-century world', *Neotest*, 34(1), pp. 1-38.

Brawley, Robert. 2014. 'Modes of objective socialization and subjective reflection in identity: Galatian identify in an imperial context' in Brian Tucker and Coleman Barke (eds.), *The T & T Clark handbook to social identity in the New Testament*. New York: Bloomsbury T & T Clark, pp. 119-144.

Chertoff, Emily. 2017. 'Prosecuting gender-based persecution: The Islamic state at the ICC', *Yale Law Journal*, 126, pp. 1050-1117.

Crawley, Heaven. 2001a. 'Gender, persecution and the concept of politics in the asylum determination process', *Forced Migration Review*, 9, pp. 17-20.

Crawley, Heaven. 2001b. *Refugees and gender: Law and process*. Bristol: Jordan Publishing.

Davis, John. 1976. 'Some reflections on Galatians 3:28, sexual roles and biblical hermeneutics', *Journal of the Evangelical Theological Society*, 19(3), pp. 201-208.

Degner, S. C. 2001. Biblical theology, exegesis of Galatians 3:28, [online]. Available at: http://www/wlstheologia.net/mode/37.

Donovan, Richard. 2016. Biblical commentary: Galatians 3:23-29, *Sermon Writer*, [online]. Available at: https://www.sermonwriter.com/biblicalcommentary/galatians-323-29.

Eisenbaum, Pamela. 2000. 'Is Paul the father of misogyny and anti-Semitism?' *Cross Currents* 50(4), pp. 506-524.

Esler, Philip. 2014. 'An outline of social identity theory', in Brian Tucker and Coleman Barke (eds.) *The T & T Clark handbook to social identity in the New Testament*. New York: Bloomsbury T & T Clark, pp. 13-40.

Fee, Gordon. 2000. *Listening to the Spirit in the text*. Grand Rapids, MI: Eerdmans.

Fisher, Helene and Elizabeth Miller. 2019. *WWL 2019 Gender-specific religious persecution: Analysis and implications*. World Watch Research, [online]. Available at: https://bit.ly/34tqscM.

Fisher, Helene, Elizabeth Miller and Eva Mayer. 2020. *2020 Gender-specific religious persecution*. World Watch Research, [online]. Available at: https://pewrsr.ch/3nsaKao.

Freedman, Jane. 2015. *Gendering the international asylum and refugee debate*. London: Palgrave Macmillan.
Fung, Ronald. 1988. *The epistle to the Galatians*. Grand Rapids, MI: Eerdmans.
Gilbert, Lela. 2018. Gender-based violence as an expression of Christian persecution in Muslim lands. *World Watch Monitor*. Available at https://www.worldwatchmonitor.org/old-siteimages-pdfs/2533678.pdf.
Greatbach, Jacqueline. 1989. 'The gender difference: Feminist critiques of refugee discourse', *International Journal of Refugee Law* 4(1), pp. 518-27.
Grobler, Tommy. 2011. Neither male nor female: The implication of Galatians 3:26-29 for today's church. B.Th thesis, South African Theological Seminary, South Africa. Available at: https://www.sats.eduza/wp-content/uploads/2014/09/Gend----T-Bachelors-Thesis-RES4361.pdf.
Gundry-Volf, Judith. 1997. 'Christ and gender: A study of difference and equality in Gal. 3, 28' in C. Landmesser, H. J. Eckstein and H. Lichtenberger (eds.) *Jesus Christus als die Mitte der Schrift. Studien zur Hermeneutik des Evangeliums*. New York: Walter de Gruyter, pp. 439-77.
Hagglund, Amanda. 2015. Gender-related persecution of refugee women: A feminist analysis of the persecution grounds of the refugee definition. Master of Laws thesis, Faculty of Law, Lund University. Available at: https://bit.ly/2GAd1zw.
Haines, Rodger. 2003. 'Gender-related persecution' in E. Feller, V. Turk and F. Nicholson (eds.) *Refugee protection in international law: UNHCR's global consultations on international protection*. Cambridge: Cambridge University Press, pp. 319-50.
Harris, Lindsay. 2009. 'Untold stories: Gender-related persecution and asylum in South Africa', *Michigan Journal of Gender and Law* 5(2), pp. 291-347.
Hove, Richard. 1999. *Equality in Christ? Galatians 3:28 and the gender dispute*. Wheaton, IL: Crossway.
Kasomo, Daniel. 2010. 'The role of women in the church in Africa', *International Journal of Sociology and Anthropology*, 2(6), pp. 126-39.
Kelly, Nancy. 1993. 'Gender-related persecution: Assessing the asylum claims of women', *Cornell International Law Journal*, 26(3), pp. 625-74.
Kirk, Linda. 2010. *Gender-related persecution and the refugee convention*, [online]. Available at: https://bit.ly/3nx9H9l.
LaViolette, Nicole. 2008. 'Gender-related refugee claims: Expanding the slope of the Canadian guidelines', *International Journal of Refugee Law* 8, pp. 1-41. [online] Available at: https://www.uro.no/studrer/emner/jus/jus/Jur5530/v08/undervisnings_materiale/Canada.
MacArthur, John Jr. 1987. *The MacArthur New Testament Commentary: Galatians*. Chicago: Moody Bible Institute.
Marshall, Julie and Helen Barrett. 2018. 'Human rights of refugee survivors of sexual and gender-based violence with communication disability', *International Journal of Speech-Language Pathology*, 20(1), pp. 44-49.
Moore, Rebecca. 2015. *Women in Christian traditions*. New York: New York University Press.

Snodgrass, Klyne. 1986. 'Galatians 3:28: Conumdrum or solution?' in A. Mickelsen (ed.) *Women, authority and the Bible*. Downers Grove, IL: InterVarsity Press, pp. 161-81.

Tenney, Merrill. 1989. *Galatians: The charter of Christian liberty*. Grand Rapids, MI: Eerdmans.

Tolmie, Francois. 2014. 'Tendencies in the interpretation of Galatians 3:28 since 1990', *Acta Theologica*, 34(19), pp. 105-29.

UNHCR (2008) *Handbook for the protection of women and girls*. Available at: https://bit.ly/33zETfS.

Witherington, Ben. 2009. *What's in the word: Rethinking the socio-rhetorical character of the New Testament*. Waco: Baylor University Press.

Assessing the specificity of the vulnerability of girls and women belonging to religious minorities
A methodological exploration

Dennis P. Petri[1]

Abstract

Are girls and women who belong to religious minorities more vulnerable than boys and men? The answer to this question may seem obvious, but determining an objective answer would require a complex and time-consuming research design. A more pertinent and easier approach would be to seek to understand the specific vulnerabilities of religious females. To this end, I propose a methodological framework that can be used to determine the vulnerability of females belonging to religious minority groups, and I apply it to cases in Colombia, Egypt, Mexico and Syria.

Keywords Gender-based violence, religious freedom, religious vulnerability, Colombia, Egypt, Mexico, Syria.

1. Introduction

Are girls and women who belong to religious minorities more vulnerable than boys and men? The answer to this question may seem obvious. After all, since women are generally believed to be subject to physical harm, discrimination and exploitation more frequently and more severely than men – for a variety of biological, socio-cultural and political reasons – it seems likely that the vulnerability of females is greater than that of males. For example, Coptic girls in Egypt are vulnerable not only to the discrimination that affects their religious community, but also to the relative impunity with which gender-based violence is committed against its female members. The World Watch Research Unit of Open Doors International has recently issued a series of compelling reports on Nigeria, Iraq, Ethiopia, Egypt, Colombia and the Central African Republic that describe the compound vulnerability of religious affiliation and gender.[2] Other sources have also raised the issue of the intersection-

---

[1] Dennis P. Petri is scholar-at-large at the Observatory of Religious Freedom in Latin America, lecturer at The Hague University of Applied Sciences and the Universidad Latinoamericana de Ciencia y Tecnología, and director of the Foundation Platform for Social Transformation (www.platformforsocialtransformation.org). This article is taken from sections of his PhD dissertation, The Specific Vulnerability of Religious Minorities (Vrije Universiteit Amsterdam, 2020). This article uses American English. The author thanks Teresa Flores for her very helpful comments and suggestions. Article submitted: 15 June 2019, article accepted: 21 July 2020. Email: dp.petri@gmail.com.

[2] These documents can be found at http://opendoorsanalytical.org/gender-specific-persecuti-

ality of gender discrimination and religious freedom (Tadroz 2015; Mounstephen 2019; see also the article by Symes in the present volume).

Highlighting the double or compound vulnerability of girls and women does not imply, however, that they are necessarily more vulnerable to suffering human-rights abuses than men. To objectively determine this, we would need to establish the degree of vulnerability of both genders and then compare them. This is certainly not an impossible exercise, but it would require a complex and time-consuming research design.

Moreover, one might ask what added analytical value would be gained from such an effort, if the objective is to raise awareness of a problem and work towards solving it. From a humanitarian perspective, it may be sufficient, though already difficult enough in some cases, to seek a comprehensive understanding of the threats to which women and girls are vulnerable, and to research what measures can be taken to reduce their vulnerability. Similarly, from an advocacy perspective, it may not be necessary to establish which gender suffers more. Rather, making a convincing case that women and girls suffer *significantly* (instead of more than males) may be sufficient to attract the desired political attention to the plight of this particular subgroup.

Therefore, a more pertinent approach would be to seek to understand the specific vulnerabilities of religious females – i.e. to what extent their suffering is relatable to their gender in combination with their religious affiliation, why this is so and, most importantly, what can be done to help them (and consequently what should be demanded from churches, humanitarian organizations and political authorities). Not only is this task more pertinent in my view, but I also believe it is easier to accomplish.

In this article, I first propose a methodological framework that can be used to determine the specific vulnerabilities of females belonging to Christian groups. Second, I present a sampling of empirical material on the vulnerability of women that I collected in recent years in Colombia, Egypt, Mexico and Syria.[3] Third, I apply my framework to assess the vulnerabilities of these females.

2. The specificity assessment

The aim of the specificity assessment is to determine to what extent vulnerability is specific to a particular minority, such as religious girls and women, as distinguished from other groups.[4] Following the proposition that it is possible to determine em-

---

on/ (password: freedom).

[3] I collected these empirical data while working for Open Doors International (2011-2018), as doctoral researcher at Vrije Universiteit Amsterdam (2012-2020) and as director of the Observatory of Religious Freedom in Latin America (2018-2020).

[4] As is common in sociology and psychology, I define 'minority' as a social subdivision of society that is less dominant than or even subordinate to the majority, without regard to its size.

pirically the degree of specificity – defined as a condition that can be more or less particular to an individual or group – of the vulnerability of a minority, I use a three-level sliding scale (Table 1), which I justify in the subsequent narrative. To attain a more nuanced picture than would otherwise be possible, I apply the sliding scale to determine the degree of specificity of the observed minority relative to particular threats it faces, and not to its vulnerability in general.

Degree of specificity	Interpretation
Low (not very specific)	The whole population is vulnerable to this threat, including the observed minority.
Medium (quite specific)	The whole population is vulnerable to this threat, but the observed minority is particularly vulnerable.
High (very specific)	The observed minority is specifically vulnerable to this threat.

Table 1: Degree of specificity of the vulnerability of the religious minority to identified threats Source: Petri (2020).

Using a sliding scale allows us to differentiate practically between threats that are applicable only to the observed minority and those it shares with other groups. In this way, I can overcome the implicit binary approach to specificity (specific versus not specific) that characterizes most analyses of religious-freedom violations. Binary approaches to specificity are misleading in my opinion, because they cause many types of threats to which minorities are vulnerable to be discarded based on the judgement that they are 'not specific' to this group.

This exclusivity trap is further reinforced by the use of preconceived notions of what qualifies as persecution. Such notions hinder an open-ended observation of all threats to which minorities are vulnerable. As Mounstephen (2019) notes, "A reluctance to recognize the particularity of vulnerability due to religious identity and belief has been highlighted by some witnesses" who were consulted for the *Bishop of Truro's Independent Review for the Foreign Secretary of FCO Support for Persecuted Christians*. (FCO is the British Foreign and Commonwealth Office. I was among the witnesses consulted for this report.)

Readers may observe similarities between my sliding scale and the categories of pressure used in *Compound Structural Vulnerabilities Facing Christian Women*, a series of reports by the World Watch Research Unit (WWR) of Open Doors International, issued in 2018 and 2019. The similarities can be explained by the fact that I worked for WWR between 2011 and 2016 and have continued to advise the organization since then. My personal reflections on the matter were inspired by my interaction with the WWR team and have also contributed towards shaping its approach.

However, two elements differentiate my approach from WWR's. First, I focus exclusively on identifying the degree of specificity of the threats faced by women who belong to a religious minority, and I refrain from making any statement regarding their intensity in themselves or in comparison to the experience of men belonging to the same group. As argued above, establishing the specific vulnerabilities of women who belong to religious minorities is sufficient for advocacy and humanitarian purposes; there is no need to get into a controversy over whether women suffer more so then men. Second, I consider any kind of threats faced by religious women, regardless of whether there is clear direct targeting or religious persecution. To avoid the implicit connotations that the word 'persecution' carries, I deliberately avoid its use, favoring an open-ended observation of the specific vulnerabilities of religious minorities.

Bartman (2018), writing on the victimization of journalists in Mexico, confronted a similar problem that is also related to the determination of specificity. His article "undermines the official narrative that there is nothing distinct about violence against journalists, and that it is a mere corollary of crime" by proving that journalists have in fact been victims of targeted violence (and are even at a higher risk than the general population of being killed) by both organized crime and subnational government officials because of the nature of their work. My use of a sliding scale differs from but approximates Bartman's reliance on statistical probabilities. I have only three categories in the scale because the qualitative data I collected do not allow me to be more precise than that.

We must keep in mind that specificity is not the same thing as severity or intensity. To say that a threat has a low degree of specificity means only that it has a low degree of uniqueness for the observed minority, not that it is low in intensity. A threat with a low degree of specificity can be very intense, or the opposite can be true.

3. Examples of the vulnerability of women belonging to religious minorities

In this section, I present four cases of threats faced by religious women or girls in very different contexts. Since this is an exploratory study, I selected these cases based on the availability of empirical material. These cases serve primarily as illustrations of the position of women, highlighting both their vulnerability and their resilience. Due to space limitations, I cannot describe each context in depth. I discuss the specificity of these threats to women in the next section.

3.1 Reprisals for women's advocacy for freedom of education among the Nasa ethnic group in Colombia

In 2010, during a trip to Bogotá, Colombia, I met Ana Silvia Secué, an indigenous schoolteacher belonging to the Nasa ethnic group. In her interview with me, she described the violence she had suffered within her indigenous community after she decided to establish a confessional school and started an organization to advocate for the religious rights of Colombia's indigenous Christians:

> One time, guerrillas stormed into my classroom and took children to recruit them for their groups. Indigenous leaders had given them permission to do that. I never saw those children again. But I never give up and always continue and set up another school.

Christian women in the Nasa ethnic group reject traditional indigenous education and refuse to take part in traditional indigenous rituals (including traditional medicine), which they deem incompatible with their newly adopted Christian faith. This refusal has led to violent reprisals. In my interviews and in various press reports, Nasa Christian women complained regularly about the public school system in the *resguardos indígenas* (indigenous reserves), where children are required to learn about "indigenous rituals related to witchcraft," and the subsequent opposition they received from the indigenous authorities (Visión Agape 2012). One woman said:

> We [Christian women] teach them [their children] that God exists, but this bothered them [the indigenous leaders] because they are clinging onto their rituals, their customs. But the children welcomed it. We teach the children that the dignity of a person is that he is created in the image and likeness of God, not that he drinks *chicha* [a traditional alcoholic drink used in religious ceremonies], and that annoyed them.[5]

Ana Silvia actively engaged national media to denounce the treatment of indigenous Christian converts, lobbied the Colombian Congress to promote legal reforms, established connections with various national and international non-governmental organizations (NGOs) and even ran for a senatorial seat herself in 2014. Her (unsuccessful) senatorial campaign, which revolved around her demands for freedom of education, caused her to be threatened with torture on several occasions by the indigenous authorities. In my interviews with her, Ana Silvia indicated that her training in civic rights has helped her develop and carry out her educational and

---

[5] Interview with María Teresa Mesa, 2013.

political initiatives. Thanks to a basic understanding of the law, she said, she has been able to fight legal battles and advocate for the rights of Nasa Christians before the national government.

In practice, however, the rights of Christian indigenous women (and, generally speaking, of religious minorities) are undermined by the broad legal protection granted to indigenous self-determination rights (Scolnicov 2011; Pinto 2015; Petri 2020). Here, it is necessary to confront the frequently heard charge that the language of justice and human rights is a form of Western and colonial imposition that is incompatible with the norms of traditional cultures. As Martha Nussbaum stresses in *Women and Human Development: The Capabilities Approach* (2000), the rejection of religious freedom, or of any other human right for that matter, by appealing to traditional cultural norms is nonsensical. Regarding discrimination against women, Nussbaum (2000:225) argues that using the notion of tradition to resist this human right is not only self-serving but also too simplistic, because it ignores the fact that cultures are dynamic and are "scenes of debate and contestation," which include dominant voices but also voices of women (and, by extension, any vulnerable group) "which have not always been heard." In other words, if one wishes to appeal to tradition, one must also be willing to listen to the non-dominant voices that are part of this tradition. In a similar vein, Toft (2016) argues that because "the human rights regime has undergone a systematic diffusion across the world," depicting it as a Western imposition is both incorrect and a "denial of agency" of vulnerable communities.

3.2 Discrimination against Coptic girls in Egypt[6]

Violence against women is a major issue in Egypt, as reported by many human-rights organizations (Human Rights Watch 2013; Amnesty International 2015). It is even more severe for Coptic girls and is often related to kidnappings and forced conversion (Fox 2008:237). Researcher Magdy Khalil stated:

> Abducting and converting Coptic girls to Islam is not only a result of the paranoid and racist incitation against the Copts, it is an organized and pre-planned process by associations and organizations inside Egypt with domestic and Arab funding, as the main role in seducing and luring Coptic girls is carried through cunning, deceit, and enticement, or through force if required. (AINA News, 2009)

The abduction of Coptic girls increased after the January 2011 revolution as Islamist groups became increasingly visible (Marshall, Gilbert and Shea 2013). Accord-

---

[6] Some of the interviews quoted in this section were conducted by my colleague Markus Tozman and used with his permission.

ing to accounts, an increasing number of Coptic girls were abducted and forced into Islamic marriages after the initial January 25 revolution: "Salafis know who is part of their group and [who is] not. They will do whatever they want with the others. They would select women to abduct and forcefully convert to Islam or rape on the spot and nobody would interfere."[7]

Coptic women constantly feel the threat of gender-based violence, including the obligation to wear the Islamic veil.[8] As one interviewee put it, "the double vulnerability of Christian women lies partly in the fact that they are being considered infidels and an enticement to men because they go unveiled."[9] This double vulnerability is greater for the lower social classes, as Tozman (2013:3) noted, because they have more limited resources to defend themselves in the face of discrimination, economic hardships and sectarian violence. A Coptic historian declared:

> [An Egyptian citizen with full citizenship rights] has to be Sunni not Shia, has to have a certain income bracket, fully supportive of the state. ... The discourse of discrimination is always based on class, race and then sexuality. Classes are dominant here, and then you can further dissect this. So if you talk about Egypt, probably the worst case of citizen to be is a disabled, homosexual, lower class, with a different ethnicity. But at the macro level, the largest aspect of discrimination would be based on class.[10]

Discrimination against Copts in the job market occurs primarily when with regard to public-sector jobs but also in the business sphere: "Even in the private sectors, there are companies that do not employ Christians at all. Those companies most probably are owned by leading figures of the Muslim Brotherhood and other Islamist figures" (Thabet 2014:6). The same is true for appointments in media organizations. This situation affects all Copts, but women in particular: "Especially, women in the workplace experience discrimination and hostilities. A competent Christian woman engineer was denied promotion because Muslim male colleagues would not want to work under a Christian woman. A single Christian nurse had to stop working because Muslims did not want her to help them. Her employers did not support her."[11]

---

[7] Interview with Magda Ramzy, 2013.
[8] Interviews with Magdy Aziz Tobia, Marian, Casper Wuite and Moudi Fayek, 2013.
[9] Interview with Miriam van Norden, 2014.
[10] Interview with Karim Maged Malak, 2013.
[11] Interview with Miriam van Norden, 2014.

The complicity of the police and the impunity with which people committed violence against Copts were illustrated by the testimony of a Coptic woman who was beaten by the military and never received justice:

> For weeks, you could see the bruises on my body. When I went to the doctor for a physical examination, I was humiliated and harassed. I had no case to file against the soldiers, the police told me. I had to prove they had done this to me. Even after I had filed a report with proof of my bruises and eyewitness testimonies, I was pressed to give up my case. In the end, after a prolonged period of pressure and bullying, I gave up, realizing that I would not receive justice. As a Christian woman, I simply did not have the power and was not taken seriously and even threatened.[12]

3.3 Abduction of Christian girls by drug cartel violence in Mexico

Many areas of Mexico have recently experienced a particularly fierce upsurge of cartel-related violence (Schedler 2015; Rosen and Zepeda 2016). This violence affects the population in general, including Christian women. A particularly cruel account was shared by an evangelical pastor in a crime-torn city in the northwestern state of Tamaulipas:

> A pastor friend of mine was abducted by a criminal gang that was part of a satanic cult. His family was ordered to pay a ransom. His wife and family succeeded in collecting the money and the criminals came to take it. The pastor's wife asked them, "But where is my husband?" "He is at the beginning of your street," they told her. When she went there, her husband was there. Only he was not alive. She found him in a plastic garbage bag, killed and hacked into pieces.[13]

Even though strong religious faith may increase resilience by fostering increased self-awareness, it does not necessarily guarantee protection. Nevertheless, in my interview it became clear that Christian women with strong religious convictions had grown in courage and were often more able to defend themselves against threats. I interviewed one girl who had been kidnapped by Los Zetas, a particularly cruel drug cartel that adheres to a satanic cult called Santa Muerte (Holy Death). She explained:

> I was abducted along with other people by Los Zetas because I happened to witness one of their raids. I had every reason to fear for my life and that of my 10-year-old niece who was abducted as well. But I stood up and took authority. I told them, "I

---

[12] Interview with Sara, 2014.
[13] Identities of the interviewees have been kept confidential for their protection. Demographic details and transcripts of each interview are available from the author on request.

am a Christian, you are not going to rape me. You are not allowed. You are going to release me and my niece, and you are going to give us food. I also want you to take off all your Santa Muerte amulets." Amazingly enough, they all did what I said. I prayed with these men and all the people abducted. Nothing happened to us, and after three days, my niece and I were released!

I received similar testimonies from other interviewees. One source shared that a friend abducted by Los Zetas was released when they learned he was a Christian. A girl who had also been kidnapped by Los Zetas stated, "They were going to shoot me, but something happened with the gun they were using because the bullet did not come out. One of Los Zetas told his partners to release me, saying that no one could touch this girl because God was with her." It appears that Los Zetas have some degree of respect for religion, possibly because many of them are extremely superstitious, as illustrated by their attachment to the Santa Muerte cult. Some interviewees also indicated that some gang members were raised in Christian families and continue to hold the religion in esteem, despite their criminal involvement. In most cases, however, this does not happen, and it appears that most criminals have no respect whatsoever for religion and religious institutions.

3.4 Sexual abuse of Christian women in Syria[14]

"Young unmarried women are directly threatened by kidnappings and rape," a Syrian refugee told Swedish journalist Nuri Kino (2013:7). Within a context of impunity and absence of rule of law, women are increasingly vulnerable to sexual abuse. In the conflict, Christian women are doubly vulnerable: "Women in general – particularly Christians – have become easy targets for male criminals" (Kino 2013:18). Open Doors field reports described the tragic case of one Christian girl from the Tabaleh area of Damascus who was kidnapped in 2012 and later found in a house with other women in a 'freedom fighter' area where she was used as a sex prize after their fighting. After she was returned home, she committed suicide.

The sexual assaults on women may or may not have a religious (Islamist) motive, but it can be assumed that they are enabled by the widespread impunity for such crimes. Some Muslim clerics have even offered theological justifications of rape, issuing several fatwas that authorized the rape of non-Sunni women and even speaking of a 'sexual jihad' (A Big Message 2013). In 2013, a Jordanian Salafi sheikh issued a fatwa on YouTube "declaring that it is lawful for opponents of the regime of Bashar al-Assad to rape 'any Syrian woman not Sunni [including Alawites, Druze and Christians]'" (Independent Catholic News 2013; Ibrahim 2013).

---

[14] This section contains edited excerpts from Pastoor (pseudonym) (2013).

4. Application of the specificity assessment

I will now assign a degree of specificity to each of the four threats to girls and women discussed in the previous section (Table 2).

Case	Degree of specificity
Reprisals for women's advocacy for freedom of education amongst the Nasa ethnic group in Colombia	Low
Discrimination against Coptic girls in Egypt	Medium
Abduction of Christian girls by drug cartel violence in Mexico	Low
Sexual abuse of Christian women in Syria	Medium

Table 2: Specificity assessment of threats against identified religious female subgroups

None of the threats was assigned a high degree of specificity, because none of these threats apply exclusively to Christian women. In other words, other groups, including men belonging to the same religious group or women belonging to other religious (or non-religious) groups, may face the same threats.

Nevertheless, these threats present some unique features directly related to the gender and religious affiliation of the women they affect. For example, discrimination against Coptic girls in Egypt was rated at a medium degree of specificity, because violence against women is an issue throughout Egyptian society but Coptic girls (and possibly girls belonging to other religious minorities) are specifically vulnerable to this threat, especially since crimes against them are committed with widespread impunity.

I applied a similar reasoning to the sexual abuse of Christian women in Syria. The threat of sexual abuse applies to women in Syrian society generally, but it especially affects girls from non-Sunni religions, including Christianity. Whether Christian girls are more affected by this threat than girls belonging to other non-Sunni religions cannot be determined from the available information.

The threat against advocates for freedom of education in Colombia was rated at a low degree of specificity. This behavior in which the indigenous Christian women are engaging is a direct extension of their religious convictions, since they view both indigenous rituals and indigenous education as things to avoid. The threats they face as a result of this stance could also apply to other non-Christian indigenous groups or individuals should they defy the political authority of the *resguardos indígenas*.

Finally, the threat of abduction of Christian girls by Mexican drug cartels, although very intense, was given a low degree of specificity, because it affects the whole Mexican population to a similar extent. Indeed, amidst the current upsurge of cartel-related violence, kidnap-for-ransom activities affect broad segments of society. However, the Christian convictions of the abducted girls are an important part of their testimony.

5. Concluding remarks

Implicit in many studies of religious freedom is the notion that a particular incident should only be considered as religious persecution if it applies exclusively to a religious group (or subgroup, such as religious women in the examples I presented), a notion Marshall (2018) rejects. This preoccupation with exclusivity is both unnecessary and dangerous. It is unnecessary because from a humanitarian or advocacy perspective, it is most important to plausibly establish that girls and women are affected by a particular threat, which should be enough to qualify the concern as structural and deserving urgent attention.

The preoccupation with exclusivity is also dangerous because it causes violations of religious freedom that have lower degrees of specificity to be overlooked. Indeed, it can have disastrous consequences if governments and relief agencies focus only on threats with a high degree of specificity, because this leads to the neglect of severe threats such as the Colombian and Mexican cases I discussed above. In my advocacy work for religious freedom, I have heard government officials use the argument that a particular human-rights violation cannot be qualified as 'religious' or as 'persecution,' which then becomes a justification for not acting on it.

The very fact that the Middle Eastern cases may be more familiar to the reader than the Latin American cases is likely related to the fact that the latter group is generally not considered as constituting violations of religious freedom. To be fair, observing gender discrimination committed for religious reasons in Latin America is particularly complex, because it is a majority-Christian continent with a predominant culture characterized by machismo. But this complexity only underscores the importance of taking the specificity of the threats affecting women into account.

To overcome this conceptual issue, the methodological innovation of the specificity assessment proposed in this paper consists in adopting a sliding scale instead of the implicit binary approach that many seem to follow. This sliding scale enables us to consider degrees of specificity rather than falling into the exclusivity trap and discarding threats that are deemed, for arbitrary reasons, 'not specific enough' or not religious persecution.

References

A Big Message. 2013. 'Tunisia – Teenage girls going to Syria in response to alleged fatwa on sexual jihad'. 2 April 2013.

AINA News. 2009. 'Egyptian security refuses to return abducted Christian Coptic girl', 18 July 2009. Available at: http://www.aina.org/news/20090718111414.htm.

Amnesty International. 2015. *Amnesty International Annual Report 2014/2015*. London: Amnesty International. Available at: https://www.amnesty.org/en/latest/research/2015/02/annual-report-201415/.

Bartman, Jos Midas. 2018. 'Murder in Mexico: Are Journalists Victims of General Violence or Targeted Political Violence?' *Democratization* 25(7), pp. 1093-1113.

Fox, Jonathan 2008. *A World Survey of Religion and the State*. New York: Cambridge University Press.

Human Rights Watch (HRW). 2013. *World Report 2013*. New York: Human Rights Watch.

Ibrahim, Raymond. (2013) 'New fatwa permits rape of non-Sunni women in Syria', *myIslam*, 2 April 2013, [online]. Available at: https://bit.ly/3lllfKN.

Independent Catholic News. 2013. 'Syria: Christians flee rebel areas as fatwa authorizes rape of non-Sunni women', [online]. Available at: https://www.indcatholicnews.com/news/22286.

Kino, Nuri. 2013. 'Between the Barbed Wire', [online]. Available at: http://www.aina.org/reports/bbw.pdf.

Marshall, Paul A. 2018. 'Politicizing Religion', Hudson Institute [online]. Available at: https://www.hudson.org/research/14598-politicizing-religion.

Marshall, Paul A., Lela Gilbert and Nina Shea. 2013. *Persecuted: The Global Assault on Christians*. Nashville: Thomas Nelson.

Mounstephen, Philip. 2019. *Bishop of Truro's Independent Review for the Foreign Secretary of FCO Support for Persecuted Christians. Final Report and Recommendations*. Available at: https://bit.ly/3d5vnnR.

Nussbaum, Martha C. 2000. *Women and Human Development: The Capabilities Approach*. New York: Cambridge University Press.

Open Doors International, (World Watch Research Unit). 2018, 2019. *Compound Structural Vulnerabilities Facing Christian Women* (series of reports on Iraq, Ethiopia, Egypt, Colombia, Central African Republic and Nigeria), [online]. Available at: http://opendoorsanalytical.org/gender-specific-persecution/.

Pastoor, D. (pseudonym) 2013. *Vulnerability Assessment of Syria's Christians*. Harderwijk, the Netherlands: Open Doors International, World Watch Research Unit.

Petri, Dennis P. 2020. *The Specific Vulnerability of Religious Minorities*. PhD (Doctoral dissertation). Amsterdam: Vrije Universiteit Amsterdam.

Pinto, Meital. 2015. 'The Right to Culture, the Right to Dispute, and the Right to Exclude: A New Perspective on Minorities within Minorities', *Ratio Juris*, 28(4), pp. 521-39.

Rosen, Jonathan D., and & Zepeda, Roberto. 2016. *Organized Crime, Drug Trafficking, and Violence in Mexico: The Transition from Felipe Calderón to Enrique Peña Nieto*. Lanham, MD: Lexington Books.

Schedler, Andreas. 2015. *En la niebla de la guerra: los ciudadanos ante la violencia criminal organizada*. Mexico City: CIDE.

Scolnicov, Anat. 2011. *The Right to Religious Freedom in International Law. Between Group Rights and Individual Rights*. London: Routledge.

Tadros, Mariz. 2015. 'International Women's Day: Solidarity & Iraqi Religious Minority Women', Institute of Development Studies. Available at: https://bit.ly/2GNufsX.

Thabet, E. A. M. 2014. 'On the Social-Exclusion of the Christian Minority in Egypt', Paper presented at Vrije Universiteit Amsterdam, 28 October 2014.

Toft, Monica D. 2016. 'Is Religious Freedom a Western Imposition?' *Current History*, 115(777), pp. 32-35.

Tozman, M. 2013. *Mubarak, Mursi and Moslem Brotherhood: Egypt's revolution and its socioeconomic impact on the country's Christians*. Harderwijk, the Netherlands: Open Doors International/World Watch Research Unit.

Visión Agape. 2012. *The Indigenous women of Cauca's Nasa People*. Internal report. 17 June 2012.

Christians under Pressure: Studies in Discrimination and Persecution 1

Bernhard Reitsma (Ed.)

Fruitful Minorities

*The Witness and Service of
Christian Communities in
Predominantly Islamic Societies*

VKW

Left behind
An analysis of the United Nations' response to the intersecting identities of gender and religion
Rebecca Symes[1]

Abstract

Intersectional language is increasingly incorporated into the policy dialogue, analysis and reporting of UN entities and special rapporteurs including UN Women and Freedom of Religion and Belief (FoRB). This paper analyses the United Nations' responses to gendered religious persecution based on a quantitative content analysis of UN documents and a series of qualitative interviews with experts. The findings suggest that the UN is inconsistent in its recognition of the intersectional vulnerability of gender and religious persecution. Significantly, various international declarations issued by UN Women, a branch dedicated to gender equality and protection, have progressively stopped mentioning this intersection.

Keywords Religious persecution, United Nations, gender, women, intersectionality, vulnerability, human rights.

1. Introduction

More than 80 percent of the world's population has a religious affiliation (Pew Research Center 2012; Pew Research Center 2016). Religious persecution is a severe problem across the world; in fact, a recent examination of 193 UN member states has noted a marked increase in instances of religious persecution and restrictions of religious freedom (Pew Research Center 2018; Open Doors 2018). This persecution is not gender-blind. It creates a particularly high-risk environment for women who experience persecution acutely, in ways that severely violate their rights (Rees 2019; Fisher and Miller 2018).

The theory of intersectionality is a valuable tool to identify the most vulnerable people, as it considers the numerous overlapping factors of a person's identity, which exposes inequalities and subordination. Notably, this theory can be applied to the experiences of women who are strategically targeted and oppressed due to

---

[1] Rebecca Symes has worked as an independent researcher for Open Doors International and as a consultant for a project commissioned by the UK Foreign and Commonwealth Office Fund for Religious Freedom regarding gender and religious persecution. This article is taken from her completed research thesis at the University of Exeter and her presentation to the UK Foreign and Commonwealth Office review on the UN's response to religious persecution. This article uses British English spelling. Article received: 15 June 2019; accepted: 21 July 2020. Email: becca.symes97@gmail.com.

their religious affiliation. The United Nations claims to include an intersectional scope in its establishment of human-rights norms and policy-making (Campbell 2016; Fukuda-Parr 2019). Member states have committed to the 2030 Agenda for Sustainable Development and the Sustainable Development Goals (SDGs), where intersectional factors leading to discrimination are specifically included to identify the areas whereby people are left behind (UN Department of Economic and Social Affairs [DESA] 2018). The pledge to "leave no one behind" refers to the call for member states to regard the needs of the most disadvantaged, marginalized and vulnerable as a priority (Cochrane 2018). However, religion is not included here as an intersectional vulnerability factor. This omission leaves these vulnerable women unaccounted for, as they are excluded from associated analyses, dialogue and policies (Randel and German 2017; UN Women 2015). This is part of a pattern of omission throughout international policies, which indicates that the international community has yet to have fully understood and "adequately addressed" religious persecution (Ochab 2018; Mountstephen 2019). Without adequate recognition of the heightened exposure to harm that results from the intersection of religious persecution and gender, these women are indeed being left behind.

Using quantitative content analyses of UN documents, this paper exposes inconsistencies between how the UN Special Rapporteurs for freedom of religion or belief, or FoRB (on behalf of the Human Rights Council), and the UN Women documents and declarations on gender protection are recognizing this increasingly apparent intersectional vulnerability. Qualitative interviews with experts in the field deepen this analysis, drawing the conclusion that women facing this intersection are not currently consistently recognized or adequately protected by the UN. It is recommended that the platforms of the 2020 SDGs and Beijing Declaration reviews should be used to address this intersectional gap. Moreover, advocacy groups should work together with government policy-makers to ensure that this intersection is recognized as a vulnerability. I hope that these findings will help to lay a foundation for future research, policy suggestions and programming so as to protect vulnerable women.

2. Background: understanding the UN's approach to the intersectional vulnerabilities of gendered religious persecution

2.1 Why should we use an intersectional analytical lens to understand the experiences of women who face discrimination and inequality?

Intersectionality provides an analytical lens that allows for greater insight into the experiences of women who belong to persecuted religions. Intersectionality insists on considering numerous identities, to expose vulnerabilities and subordination as they intersect (Davis 2015:207). The theory moves away from viewing identities as isolated analytical categories that cause discrimination; instead, it exposes concurrent intersecting experiences of oppression, such as black women's concurrent experience of both racism and sexism (Crenshaw 1991; Sigle-Rushton 2013). An understanding of the nuanced multi-dimensional experiences of discrimination is widely considered necessary to address inequalities facing individuals (Chow 2016). Therefore, international human-rights mechanisms and policy agreements on non-discrimination laws are increasingly incorporating an intersectional analysis into policy-making. Despite the complexities of addressing the oppression of individuals in global policy, intersectionality remains a critical tool for the design and application of non-discrimination laws and equality policy, as it enables a specific understanding of discrimination (Crenshaw 1991; Quinn 2016). Therefore, intersectionality is a hugely important, complex analytical theory that highlights unseen areas of discrimination for women.

2.2 What do we already know about the intersectionality of gendered religious persecution?

Religious persecution is a severe problem across the world, and the women belonging to these groups often experience this persecution acutely and in unique ways (Ghanea 2004; Rees 2019). Religious persecution creates a particularly high-risk environment for the violation of women's rights through, for example, a lack of socio-legal protection and an elevated vulnerability to sexual violence, abduction and forced marriage (Fisher and Miller 2018). Therefore, religious persecution should be considered with an intersectional understanding, as women are deliberately and strategically targeted to pressure and break down religious communities (Fisher and Miller 2018; Jackson 2017; Tadros 2015; Barkindo et al 2013). The lens of intersectionality provides a focused analysis of the specific violence and discrimination faced by women belonging to religions experiencing persecution.

Despite this trend, religion is often left out of academic discussions of intersectionality and consequently, the international policies that list the intersecting identities of women seldom include religion (Weber 2015; Barkindo et al 2013; UN Women 2015). UN reports and literature regarding such events as Boko Haram's abduction of Christian girls in northern Nigeria or the systematic abduction and abuse of Christian and Yazidi women in Iraq by the Islamic State do not highlight the specific intersectional relationship of gender and religion (UNICEF 2018; Barkindo et al 2013; Tadros 2015). As a result, these specific vulnerabilities are largely unexplored and under-represented in policies, despite appearing to be a clear intersectional factor which heightens a woman's vulnerability (Ghanea 2017; Tadros 2015; Goss-Alexander 2018).

2.3 Why is the appreciation of this intersection in FoRB insufficient to address the vulnerability?

The FoRB section of the UN recognizes that women of religious minorities face systematic intersectional discrimination around the world (Winkler and Satterthwaite 2017). In response, the Human Rights Council has mandated the current FoRB Special Rapporteur "to continue to apply a gender perspective" in identifying "gender-specific abuses" in their reports, and two FoRB reports have specifically highlighted the intersectional vulnerability of women and religion (Office of the High Commissioner for Human Rights [OHCHR] 2019). However, the role of the FoRB Special Rapporteur is only to investigate and monitor situations and recommend solutions relating to this specific mandate. It does not possess the power to grant protection to people with religious beliefs as a human right (OHCHR 2019; Bielefeldt 2013; Ghanea 2017).

In addition, internationally recognized norms, such as Article 18 of the Universal Declaration of Human Rights, which promotes religious freedom and tolerance, are not legally binding on states (Bielefeldt 2013). Therefore, given the limited protection of FoRB in the UN, these women must seek protection through other channels of the UN that could protect and enforce their rights. Despite the appreciation of this intersection in FoRB reports, gender and religious identities are not currently translating into other spheres of the UN.

2.4 How is this intersection addressed by the UN Women?

UN bodies are increasingly referring to intersectionality in policy-making initiatives (Davis 2015; Chow 2016). An intersectional understanding has been included in the influential 2030 SDGs' "leave no one behind" agenda, to reveal the gaps where women are disadvantaged and face discrimination (Winkler and Satterthwaite 2017; Fukuda-Parr 2019; UN Women 2015; Davis 2015; UN DESA 2018; Randel and German 2017). However, religion is not included in this list of intersectional identities, which results in additional marginalization (Randel and German 2017; UN Women 2015). Even though the UN has a strong intersectional framework regarding equality, there has not been reciprocal interest between FoRB and UN Women in the intersection concerning religion (Ghanea 2017; Bielefeldt 2013).

Scholars have highlighted the pattern of omission of religion in international relations and policy. One reason suggested for this omission is the UN's limited ability to accommodate the complexities regarding seemingly conflicting rights such as gender and religion (UN DESA 2018; Chow 2016; Fukuda-Parr 2019). The international human rights bodies within the UN, such as UN Women, advocate for the rights of women to be free from impositions by religious traditions and practices (Ghanea 2017; Weber 2015). Spivak (2012) suggests that the lack of mention of religion other than in FoRB dialogues is due to the increasing secularism within the UN. Nevertheless, there appears to be inconsistency in how different elements of the UN identify women and religion. Significantly, UN Women does not include religion in its intersectional vulnerability lens, leading to a "serious protection gap" regarding the specific human-rights abuses they experience (Bielefeldt 2013:2; Ghanea 2017).

2.5 Conclusions from a review of available literature

Further investigation is needed concerning the effective use of international policies to protect women who belong to religions that face persecution. Religious persecution is not gender-blind and creates an increasingly high-risk environment for the violation of women's rights. Perpetrators of persecution may intentionally target women to incapacitate a faith community, exploiting women's lack of socio-legal protections and their elevated vulnerability to sexual violence. Despite such threats, this intersectionality has not consistently generated high-level dialogue and political will across the UN. This paper seeks to contribute towards understanding the apparent inconsistency between FoRB and UN Women and whether it results in women being left behind.

3. Research method

This study applied both quantitative and qualitative analysis to build an understanding of the extent to which the UN is recognizing the intersectionality of gender and religion. The quantitative content analysis quantified the degree to which UN FoRB and UN Women documents represented this intersection. The qualitative expert interviews explained the findings and widened the scope of the recommendations considered. This method of triangulation provided more comprehensive data and mitigated some of the limitations of the methodology (Bekhet and Zauszniewski 2012; Bryman 2016).

3.1 Content analysis

I conducted a content analysis of the annual reports of the Special Rapporteur for FoRB from 1995 to 2018 and of UN Women declarations. The aim of this analysis was to establish whether there is a broad pattern in how the UN sections have addressed the topic over time. The quantitative content analysis allowed a more systematic and replicable investigation into the extent to which the documents address the relevant concerns (Krippendorff 2004:10; Neuendorf and Kumar 2015).

The annual reports of the special rapporteur for FoRB are considered the "strongest mechanisms that FoRB has to generate new synergies" (Ghanea 2017:6; OHCHR n.d.). Each annual report was analysed independently, based on the four

Interviewee 1	Partnerships Developer & Academic Lecturer in Theology of Suffering & Persecution and Founding director of Gender and Religious Freedom.
Interviewee 2	Senior Global Gender Persecution Specialist and women's strategist for International NGO.
Interviewee 3	United Nations Representative for an international NGO.
Interviewee 4	Executive Editor & Director for human rights online newspaper specialising on religious persecution.
Interviewee 5	Research Coordinator at UNICEF and Managing Editor of the International Journal of Transitional Justice.
Interviewee 6	Senior Advisor for Social Justice and on the UN Faith advisory council

main terms of gender, sex, women and girls; moreover, during the initial reading of the annual reports, further categories were added to obtain a more accurate record. This approach mitigates the criticism that terms used in the reports may have changed over time (Krippendorff 2004). To account for the documents varying in length, the occurrence of the word list was divided by the total number of lines in each document to find the average frequency to create an overall trend. The percentage of lines relating to the topic of women in the whole document indicated the degree to which the FoRB documents highlighted the unique experiences of women in the context of religious persecution over time.

Second, the same method was applied to understand how religion has been covered in UN Women declarations. This method was applied to seven critical international agreements from 1995 to 2015, which act as "guiding documents" for the UN's understanding and creation of norms for women's equality and protection (UN Women 2019). Again, the word list was based on four main terms (religion, belief, spiritual and faith), and more categories were added as they appeared. The average frequency percentage created an overall trend of how often religion was included across the seven documents.

Simply calculating the frequency of terms appearing in the documents offered a shallow analysis (Krippendorff 2004). Therefore, to gain a better understanding of the contexts in which religion is addressed by the UN Women documents, I categorized each reference to the topic and then calculated the percentage of appearances for each category. For this purpose, I compared the Beijing Declaration and Platform for Action (United Nations 1995) with Sustainable Development Goal 5 on Gender Equality (2015). I chose these documents because UN Women (United Nations 2015) refers to them as fundamental policy frameworks for the "empowerment of women and girls." Additionally, 2020, which marks the 25th and 5th years of these documents' existence, respectively, was regarded as a "pivotal year for the accelerated realization of gender equality" (UN Women n.d.).

3.2 Qualitative interviews

Qualitative interviews complemented the quantitative content analysis data by providing possible explanations for the findings from experts working in related fields of study. The aim of the interviews was to explore the interviewees' understanding of how the UN is responding to the intersecting identities of gender and religion and to develop further areas for research (Kvale 1996).

In the selection of interviewees, I made a conscious attempt to cover a range of professional backgrounds pertinent to this topic, including NGOs, religious persecution specialists, social justice advocates and UN liaisons, to ensure a broad picture and consider different perspectives. The interviews were conducted over Skype or in person at the UN Commission of the Status of Women in March 2019, lasting about 30 minutes each. The semi-structured approach allowed each interviewee to speak in his or her area of expertise. By closely reading the transcripts, I coded the themes that emerged into the categories described in the findings below.

4. Quantitative findings

4.1 How frequently are women referred to in FoRB reports?

Each annual report discusses the themes of religious persecution observed by the Special Rapporteur for that year. Therefore, the increase in the mention of gender reflects the Special Rapporteur's growing awareness that women face specific discrimination. Figure 1 shows a significant increase in the average frequency with which women were referenced in the documents beginning in 1998. Although the figure does not show steady growth, there was a clear increase across the time span. In other words, acts of religious intolerance specifically against women were increasingly recognized in these reports.

4.2 Religion in UN Women declarations

As Figure 2 shows, mentions of religion have tended to decrease in influential declarations on the protection and empowerment of women. There was a clear decline of 87% from 1995 to 2015.

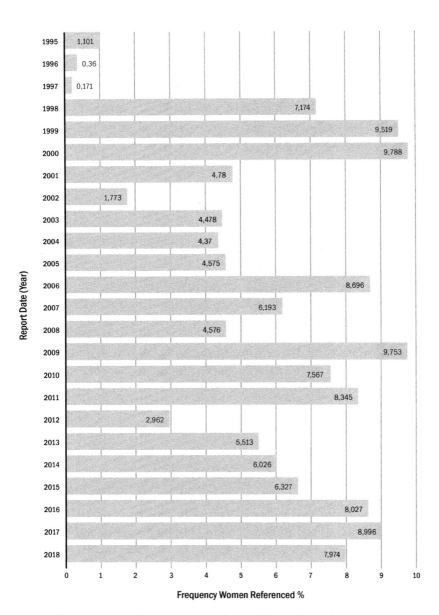

Figure 1: The frequency with which women were mentioned in UN Special Rapporteur annual reports on religious intolerance. Data was collected from 1995 to 2018. Annual reports were accessed through the archive on the Office of the High Commissioner for Human Rights' website.

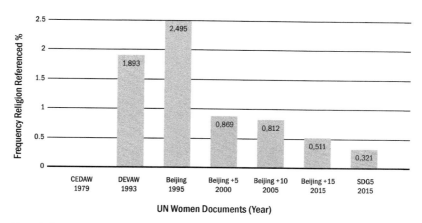

Figure 2: The frequency with which religion was mentioned in significant UN Women policy declarations. The seven documents, spanning the years from 1979 to 2015, were accessed in the UN Women archive.

4.3 Deconstruction of the mentions of religion in 1995 and 2015

Closer investigation shows that the way in which UN Women speaks about religion has shifted, from seeing it as an intersectional vulnerability towards seeing it as a source of violence against women. In the Beijing Declaration in 1995, the most common category of references to religion cited it as an intersectional factor (42%) – that is, as an aspect of identity that could result in increased discrimination and heighten a women's inequality in society. In SDG 5 in 2015, religion was referred to as an intersectional factor less frequently (15.8%). Similarly, the mentions of a woman's right to FoRB and women's increased vulnerability to religious persecution decreased from 30% in 1995 to 13% in 2015. Meanwhile, the understanding of religion as a form of violence increased from 12% in 1995 to becoming the largest category, at 43%, in 2015. This category included religion as a form of fundamentalism, or religious traditions which justify harming women and girls.

4.4 Summary

These results are significant because while persecuted women have been highlighted in UN FoRB documents as an increasingly vulnerable category, the references to them in UN Women documents are declining. Women and religion are being understood less as an intersectional vulnerability factor in UN Women documents, despite being increasingly cited in UN FoRB reports. The following qualitative analysis provides interpretation of what the UN document analysis has revealed, why the inconsistencies may arise, and the consequences for vulnerable women of a potential policy gap within the UN.

5. Qualitative findings

5.1 Recognition of religion in UN forums

Interviewee 6 (see Interviewee Table in section 3.2) remarked that the UN is attempting to become more inclusive towards religion. For example, the current UN Secretary General has established a Faith Advisory Council. However, the interviews revealed a strong theme that religion is largely absent from UN and non-governmental organization (NGO) reports on human rights. The interviewees gave three reasons for this omission. First, if UN policy-makers "do not understand religion", then it is likely to be under-represented in policy or excluded to "avoid misrepresentation" (interviewee 4). Second, interviewee 1 argued that outside of discussions on FoRB, people are "unaware" of religion as an important topic. Third, interviewee 3 stated there was not "enough political will" to achieve change regarding these issues. Conversely, interviewee 6 said, "I don't think it has [avoided] talking about religion" as "opportunities are given" to faith-based groups within the UN. Interviewee 3 concluded that there was a gap in policies for these women. Notably, they cited the UN's forum on indigenous populations for minorities as an example of how these women could potentially be protected, although further research would be needed to test whether this is a viable avenue. Other interviewees insisted on the importance of interpretation of existing polices (interviewee 6) and of the UN having a "religious understanding" (interviewee 1) when interpreting and writing policies.

5.2 Reasons for the perceived policy gap

Interviewees 1, 2, 3 and 4 highlighted the gap in UN policy regarding the intersectional vulnerability of women and religion explicitly. The intersectionality of gender and religion was viewed as "pretty ignored" (interviewee 4) throughout the UN, and no interviewee could name a policy which recognized these women. Furthermore, despite the UN FoRB Special Rapporteur report of 2013 acknowledging the protection gap, no mechanisms are in place for women seeking justice after having experienced gendered religious persecution (interviewees 2 and 5). One explanation for this problem was the lack of cooperation between the perceived competing rights" (interviewee 2). Women's rights organizations often see religious traditions and cultures as oppressive and restricting, whereas religious groups can see women's rights as hostile to their fundamental beliefs (interviewees 2 and 3). Significantly, when the two groups regard these human rights as different, the women who face this intersectional targeting "fall through a gap" of protection (interviewee 2).

One proposed solution was to help faith leaders to understand the importance of protecting women through a clearer understanding of their role in the community. Additionally, it is important for women's organizations to recognize this area of vulnerability and include it in lobbying efforts around social protection and giving women "equal voices under the law" (interviewee 2). This is particularly important within the UN, as FoRB voices are "very weak" (interviewee 3) with regard to protecting these women. Nevertheless, while a gap remains for these women, the UN is conceivably "positioned to start" including religion, given the existing frameworks of intersectionality in the UN (interviewee 3).

5.3 Limitations of the UN

The interviewees recognized that the UN has limited power to achieve protection for women who suffer religious persecution. The assumption of the UN's "relevance" (interviewee 5) in this area was challenged. Interviewee 5 remarked on the detachment of the UN, which is prone to "create categories higher up" which "don't make sense on the ground". Furthermore, the need for the cooperation of member states highlights the UN's limited power (interviewees 3, 4, 5 and 6). This is because policies are implemented by the countries that sign the declarations, not by the UN itself.

Because of the UN's limited power to ensure the implementation and enforcement of policies, the importance of civil-society, government, and grassroots cooperation (interviewees 2, 3 and 5, respectively) was highlighted as integral for achieving change. However, the UN remains a significant mechanism in providing accountability for governments (interviewee 3), funding operations (interviewee 5) and setting international norms (interviewee 6).

In sum, the interviewees largely agreed that there was an existing gap in UN policy regarding the intersectional vulnerability of women facing religious persecution. However, they also highlighted the limitations of the UN alone to address this gap.

6. Discussions of the UN's response

6.1 The UN policy gap

The quantitative findings demonstrated that the frequency with which UN Women declarations mentioned religion declined by 87% during the period from 1995 to 2015. Significantly, a comparison of Figures 1 and 2 shows that the increase in mentions of women in UN reports on FoRB was roughly inversely proportional to the decrease in the mentions of religion in UN Women documents. Therefore, it appears that the UN is inconsistent in how it addresses this intersection, and the reports of the Special Rapporteur for FoRB are not being transferred to other UN bodies. Interviewee 5 suggested that this could be because the "UN is very siloed in how it operates, and it finds it incredibly difficult to cross over." Nevertheless, the decline in acknowledgement of religion as a vulnerability could lead to a protection gap. Notably, the influential SDG 5 and the "leave no one behind" initiative, intended to "achieve gender equality and empower all women and girls," do not include the intersection of religion (UN Women 2015; Davis 2015; Winkler and Satterthwaite 2017; UN DESA 2018; Randel and German 2017). The findings from 5.1 concerning the recognition of religion in UN forums mirrors the literature, which claimed that religion is increasingly associated with infractions against the rights of women (Ghanea 2017; Chow 2016). The perception of religion and gender as 'competing rights' can result in these women falling through a protection gap (interviewee 2; Chow 2016; Fukuda-Parr 2019). Indeed, these women are not protected by the norms of FoRB, nor are they accounted for in policies on women's equality (interviewees 2 and 3; Bielefeldt 2013).

The interviewees agreed that they were aware of no existing policies that explicitly recognized these women. They suggested other avenues, however, which could account for these women facing this intersection even in the absence of policies explicitly referring to them. The interpretation of policies is important, meaning that people implementing these policies on the ground need to understand this intersectional area (interviewees 1 and 6). However, without an acknowledgement outside of FoRB, it is unclear how these interpretations might come to include these women. Notably, the interviewees cited the Universal Periodic Review process as a potential platform in which governments are held accountable for improving their record on human rights (OHCHR 2019; interviewees 3 and 4).

Despite the inclusion of religion in FoRB reports, the more influential declarations relating to women's protection do not consider this intersection. Both the lack of consistency in addressing the issue within the UN and the difficulty of implementation without member state cooperation call into question the presumption that the UN is the strongest mechanism by which to address the synergies concerning this intersection. The interviews emphasized the importance of grassroots, civil-society, and government support and participation in effecting change.

6.2 Limitations of the analyses

Before I turn to recommendations, I should mention some limitations of this research. The qualitative expert interviews allowed further elaboration of the findings and widened the scope of the recommendations considered (Bryman 2016). However, one limitation was that although they came from different professions, all the interviewees were women of faith with a particular interest in this area and who believed that a policy gap existed. More interviews, with a greater number of experts expressing a wider range of viewpoints on this subject, would have broadened the perspective. In addition, interviewing the Special Rapporteur for FoRB would have provided clearer insight into the effects of the annual reports. The research did not consider other sources or case studies of countries where the intersection of gender-based and religious targeting is occurring, as the research focus was specifically on the UN. Finally, direct engagement with women facing this intersection of threats would provide important insights into whether and specifically how they consider themselves to be left behind.

6.3 Recommendations

The rapidly changing narrative on these issues is influencing the implications of the research results and recommendations for policy and practice, as governments continue to react to events and societal pressures. FoRB and gender are increasingly being placed on the global agenda; for instance, the Ministry of Foreign Affairs of Denmark launched an expert consultation on FoRB, gender equality and the SDGs in March 2019, and the current UK government undertook a review of support for persecuted Christians, which led to creation of the UK FoRB Forum in 2020 (Mountstephen 2019). However, these advances are primarily thanks to the work of civil society and grassroots activists lobbying governments to increase their awareness of this vulnerable group. The UN could put greater pressure on its member states as it creates norms and frameworks for human rights. In particular, the UN Universal Periodic Reviews could include women facing religious persecution amongst the criteria on which governments report their human rights performance. This could be an effective way for the UN to challenge countries on matters of gender equality and protection from religious persecution (interviewee 4).

In addition, the UN Commission on the Status of Women may offer significant opportunities for attention to the issue, most notably the high-level reviews of the Beijing Declaration after 25 years and of the SDGs after five years. This research suggests that the intersectional identities of religious women facing discrimination should be included in the amendment of SDG 5, via the claim that these women are being left behind. The findings also suggest that UN entities should acknowledge their own inconsistencies, address silos and inform government policy-makers so that they can address the protection gap. In the absence of adequate top-down pressure from the UN to protect these women, it is imperative for civil society to work together with member state government delegations to ensure that these women are highlighted as a vulnerable group.

7. Conclusion

Despite not being listed as a vulnerability factor, the intersection of women and religious persecution has been highlighted as a concern by the UN FoRB Special Rapporteur (Bielefeldt 2013). Furthermore, the current UN Secretary General has stated the importance of understanding the "patterns of violations against ethnic and religious" minority women in Myanmar (UN 2018). Therefore, the problem appears to be a lack of coordination and consistency across UN bodies in how this intersection is regarded, rather than a lack of awareness.

Intersectionality is a critical theory to reveal the 'negative space' whereby the overlap of gender discrimination and religious persecution has heightened the vulnerability of some women (Davis 2015:209). The quantitative content analysis of UN documents in this research has exposed inconsistencies between FoRB and UN Women regarding how they are responding to the intersectional vulnerabilities of gender and religious persecution. Reasons for these inconsistencies include the "compartmentalising" (interviewee 5) of the UN and the perceived "competing rights" (interviewee 2) of gender and religion. Nevertheless, the effects of these inconsistencies for the women who fall into this intersectional gap deserve further research, as religious persecution and restrictions to freedom of belief are a rising crisis around the world.

All UN member states have adopted the 2030 Agenda and the Sustainable Development Goals (SDGs), which are influential in the establishment of human rights norms. By adopting the 2030 Agenda, member states have committed themselves to leaving no one behind. The omission of religion from the SDGs as an intersectional vulnerability factor, particularly for women, is a significant oversight which should be corrected so that these women can be officially recognized by UN member states. In addition, the lack of effective policy on FoRB should be ameliorated by a greater emphasis on the protection for women who fall into this intersection, through other UN bodies or state policies. The UN Universal Periodic Reviews could be further explored as an avenue to hold governments accountable for protecting women who face this intersectional violence. Finally, the importance of the participation of other actors alongside the UN on this issue is an important finding of the research. These vulnerable women must be recognized at all levels – global, state and civil – so that we are adequately advocating for their protection and ensuring that they are not left behind.

References

Barkindo, Atta, Benjamin Gudaku and Caroline Wesley. 2013. *Our bodies, their battle ground: Boko Haram and gender based violence against Christian women and children in North-Eastern Nigeria since 1999*. London: Nigeria's Political Violence Research Network.

Bekhet, Abir and Jaclene Zauszniewski. 2012. 'Methodological triangulation: an approach to understanding data', *Nursing Faculty Research and Publications*, 20(2), pp. 1-10.

Bielefeldt, Heiner. 2013. *Elimination of All Forms of Religious Intolerance*. Geneva: United Nations General Assembly.

Bryman, Alan. 2016. *Social Research Methods*. 5th edn. Oxford: Oxford University Press.

Campbell, Meghan. 2016. *CEDAW and Women's Intersecting Identities: A Pioneering Approach to Intersectional Discrimination*. Oxford: Oxford Human Rights Hub. Available at: https://bit.ly/34xoojP.

Chow, Pok Yin. 2016. 'Has Intersectionality Reached Its Limits? Intersectionality in the UN Human Rights Treaty Body Practice and the Issue of Ambivalence', *Human Rights Law Review*, 16(1), pp. 453-481.

Cochrane, Logan and Nitya Rao. 2018. 'Is the Push for Gender Sensitive Research Advancing the SDG Agenda of Leaving No One Behind?' *Forum for Development Studies*, 46(1), pp. 45-65.

Crenshaw, Kimberlé. 1991. 'Mapping the Margins: Intersectionality, Identity Politics, and Violence against Women of Color', *Stanford Law Review*, 43(6), pp. 1241-1299.

Davis, Aisha. 2015. 'Intersectionality and International Law: Recognizing Complex Identities on the Global Stage', *Harvard Human Rights Journal*, 28(2), pp. 205-242.

Fisher, Helene and Elizabeth Miller. 2018. *Gendered Persecution: World Watch List 2018 Analysis and Implications*. Open Doors International. Available at: https://bit.ly/33BxZGY.

Fukuda-Parr, Sakiko. 2019. 'Keeping Out Extreme Inequality from the SDG Agenda: The Politics of Indicators', *Global Policy*, 10(1), pp. 61-69.

Ghanea, Nazila. 2004. 'Human Rights of Religious Minorities and of Women in the Middle East', *Human Rights Quarterly*, 26(3), pp. 705-729.

Ghanea, Nazila. 2017. *Women and Religious Freedom: Synergies and Opportunities*. Oxford: USCIRF. Available at https://www.uscirf.gov/sites/default/files/WomenandReligiousFreedom.pdf.

Goss-Alexander, Elise. 2018. *Policy Focus: Women and Religious Freedom*. Washington, DC: USCIRF. Available at https://bit.ly/3lr4xd5.

Jackson, Olivia. 2017. *'Double Suffering' When Women Targeted Not Only for Gender, but Also Religion*, [online]. Available at: https://bit.ly/2SCaTde.

Krippendorff, Klaus. 2004. *Content Analysis: An Introduction to Its Methodology*. 2nd edn. Thousand Oaks, CA: Sage.

Kvale, Steinar. 1996. *Interviews: An Introduction to Qualitative Research Interviewing*. 1st edn. London: Sage Publications.

Ministry of Foreign Affairs of Denmark. 2019. Office of the Special Representative for Freedom of Religion or Belief, [online]. Available at: https://bit.ly/3defc7V.

Mounstephen, Philip. 2019. *Bishop of Truro's Independent Review for the Foreign Secretary of FCO Support for Persecuted Christians. Final Report and Recommendations*. Available at: https://bit.ly/3d5vnnR.

Neuendorf, Kimberly and Anup Kumar. 2015. 'Content Analysis' in Gianpietro Mazzoleni (ed.) *The International Encyclopedia of Political Communication*. Cleveland: John Wiley and Sons, pp. 1-10.

Ochab, Ewelina. 2018. 'Religious persecution: the ever-growing threat to us all', *Forbes*, [online]. Available at: https://bit.ly/2GxFOEU.

Office of the High Commissioner for Human Rights (OHCHR). 2019. *Special Rapporteur on Freedom of Religion or Belief*, [online], Available at; https://www.ohchr.org/en/issues/freedomreligion/pages/freedomreligionindex.aspx.

OHCHR Special Rapporteurs. 1995-2018. *Report of the Special Rapporteur on Religious Intolerance*. E/CN.4/. Geneva: United Nations.

OHCHR. 2019. *United Nations Human Rights Council: Universal Periodic Review*, [online]. Available at: https://www.ohchr.org/en/hrbodies/upr/pages/documentation.aspx.

Open Doors. 2019. *About the World Watch List*, [online]. Available at: https://www.opendoorsuk.org/persecution/about-wwl/.

Pew Research Center. 2012. *The global religious landscape*, [online]. Available at: https://www.pewforum.org/2012/12/18/global-religious-landscape-exec/.

Pew Research Center. 2016. *The gender gap in religion around the world*, [online]. Available at: https://pewrsr.ch/3nsaKao.

Pew Research Center. 2018. *Global uptick in government restrictions on religion in 2016*, [online]. Available at: https://pewrsr.ch/2Fa7krB.

Quinn, Gerard. 2016. 'Reflections on the Value of Intersectionality to the Development of Non-Discrimination Law', *Equal Rights Review*, 16, pp. 63-73.

Randel, Judith and Tony German. 2017. *Delivering Results to Leave No One Behind*. Paris: Development Initiatives.

Rees, Matthew. 2019. *Paying the Price Twice: How Religious Persecution Exacerbates the Vulnerabilities of Marginalised Groups*. Open Doors International World Watch Research.

Sayer, Andrew. 1992. *Method in Social Science: A Realist Approach*. 1st edn. London: Routledge.

Sigle-Rushton, Wendy. 2013. 'Intersectionality' in Mary Evans (ed.) *Gender: The Key Concepts*. Abingdon: Routledge, pp. 1-9.

Spivak, Gayatri. 2012. *An Aesthetic Education in the Era of Globalization*. Cambridge: Harvard University Press.

Tadros, Mariz. 2015. 'International Women's Day: Solidarity & Iraqi Religious Minority Women', Institute of Development Studies. Available at: https://bit.ly/2GNufsX.

UN Department of Economic and Social Affairs. 2018. *Leaving No One Behind*, [online]. Available at: https://www.un.org/development/desa/en/news/sustainable/leaving-no-one-behind.html.

UN General Assembly. 1979. *Convention on the Elimination of All Forms of Discrimination against Women*. New York: United Nations. [Resolution 34/180].

UN General Assembly. 1993. *Declaration on the Elimination of Violence against Women*. New York: United Nations. [A/RES/48/104].

UN General Assembly. 2015. *Turning Promises into Action: Gender Equality in the 2030 Agenda for Sustainable Development*. New York: United Nations. [A/RES/70/1].

UN Women. 2015. *Ending Violence against Women: From the Beijing Platform for Action to the Sustainable Development Goals*. New York: UN Women. Available at: https://bit.ly/34zYrA7.

UN Women. 2019. *About UN Women: Work and Priorities*. Available at: http://www.unwomen.org/en/about-us/about-un-women.

UN World Conference on Women. 1996. *The Beijing Declaration and the Platform for Action: Fourth World Conference on Women,* Beijing, China, 4-15 September 1995. New York, Dept. of Public Information, United Nations.

UNICEF. 2018. 'More Than 1,000 Children in North Eastern Nigeria Abducted by Boko Haram Since 2013', [online]. Available at: https://www.unicef.org/wca/press-releases/more-1000-children-northeastern-nigeria-abducted-boko-haram-2013.

Weber, Beverly. 2015. 'Gender, Race, Religion, Faith? Rethinking Intersectionality in German Feminisms', *European Journal of Women's Studies*, 22(1), pp. 22-36.

Winkler, Inga and Margaret Satterthwaite. 2017. 'Leaving No One behind? Persistent Inequalities in the SDGs', *International Journal of Human Rights*, 21(7), pp. 1073-1097.

Christine Schirrmacher

"Let there be no Compulsion in Religion" (Sura 2:256)

Apostasy from Islam as judged by contemporary Islamic Theologians

Discourses on
Apostasy,
Religious Freedom,
and Human Rights

VKW

At the crossroads of freedom of religion and women's equality rights
Some reflections from South Asia
Saumya Uma[1]

Abstract

Religion plays a positive role in society. However, in many parts of the world patriarchal forces, combined with religious fundamentalist impulses, have subverted women's equality rights. This article examines the intersections between freedom of religion and women's equality rights in South Asia, reflecting upon specific incidents and examples drawn from countries in the region. Both patriarchy and religious fundamentalism are pervasive and cannot be attributed to a specific country, region or religion but has undermined women's rights in South Asia. International human rights standards may assist in addressing such violations. There is potential for a collaborative project between religious actors and women's rights advocates.

Keywords South Asia, women's equality rights, religion, violence, discrimination, fundamentalist, patriarchy, synergy, human rights.

1. Introduction

Religion plays an important role in the lives of many individuals. It provides a sense of fulfilment of purpose in life and is a source of strength and solace in crisis situations. Shared cultural values, religious beliefs, practices and norms bind human beings together at the social level, conferring a sense of individual and collective identity. Religion has also been a source of empowerment for individuals and communities, communicating powerful messages of love, respect, dignity, peace, justice and equality. Women are no exception to this phenomenon, as they have been beneficiaries of the positive attributes of religion.

As Engels observed, "Religions are founded by people who feel a need for religion themselves and have a feeling for the religious needs of the masses" (Engels 1966:197). Socio-economic, historical and political contexts have often shaped

---

[1] Dr Saumya Uma is Associate Professor at Jindal Global Law School, O. P. Jindal Global University, Sonipat, Haryana, India. Her area of specialization is at the intersections of gender, human rights and the law. She has over 26 years of experience as an academic, law researcher, law practitioner, trainer, writer and campaigner on issues of gender, law and human rights. This article uses British English. A version of this article was presented at the Gender and Religious Freedom Consultation, Abuja, Nigeria, 28–30 March 2019. The author thanks the peer reviewers for their insightful comments and suggestions. Article received: 3 September 2019; accepted: 19 April 2020. E-mail: saumyauma@gmail.com.

religious movements. The origin of most, if not all, religions can be traced to resistance against established oppressive and exclusionary religious structures and discriminatory practices. For example, Christianity, which subsequently became the religion of the Roman empire, was initially a religion of those who were brutally oppressed and mercilessly exploited by the tyrannical rule of the Roman emperor (Engineer 1975:34). Islam began as a movement that countered hegemonic practices in pre-Islamic Arabia. In South Asia, the genesis of Sikhism can be traced to a counter-majoritarian initiative against the oppressive caste system and ritualism then prevalent in Hindu society. The caste system was categorically rejected by the first Sikh leader, Guru Nanak (see Puri 2003). However, over the centuries, once religions took root as structured institutions with rigid dogmas, fissures developed between the religious philosophy and values preached and propagated, on one hand, and ground-level practices on the other.

Globally, we have witnessed a renaissance of religious extremism, fanaticism and intolerance of individual acts of questioning, critiquing or rejecting religion – what we today refer to as religious fundamentalism (see Yilmaz 2006). This has led to a sharp polarization of communities along religious lines, accompanied by intense conflict. The forces of patriarchy, when combined with actors of religious fundamentalism within all major world religions, have resulted in oppression and alienation of women, tolerance of violence against women and, in many instances, propagation of discriminatory practices against women. The language and normative standards established by human rights documents provide a lens through which to critique this phenomenon so as to protect and promote women's human rights.

2. The South Asian context: an overview

The South Asian region, including such countries as Afghanistan, Bangladesh, Bhutan, India, the Maldives, Nepal, Pakistan and Sri Lanka, is the crucible for at least nine major world religions. These include the Baha'i faith, Buddhism, Christianity, Hinduism, Islam, Jainism, Judaism, Sikhism and Zoroastrianism. It is also the birthplace of four major religions – Hinduism, Sikhism, Buddhism and Jainism. Religious diversity and multiculturalism are the hallmark of South Asia.

Juxtaposed with this religious diversity are extensive violations of freedom of religion. Most national constitutions, with the exception of India and Nepal, accord a special status to the majority religion, either by declaring it to be the state religion or by granting it special protection. The partitioning of India, which led to the formation of Pakistan and a re-drawing of India's boundaries, and the subsequent birth of Bangladesh, have resulted in continued violation of minority rights due to Hindu–Muslim animosity (Khan and Rahman 2009:367). Religious minorities in most South Asian countries are specifically targeted for a range of discriminatory, exclusionary practices. A culture of impunity for these heinous violations is deeply entrenched within institutional structures and processes, thereby undermining the religious minority communities' access to justice.

South Asia in general, and India and Sri Lanka in particular, are also said to be new targets of the Islamic State, due to local religious fissures and imported Wahabism (Dhume 2019). The Easter Sunday attacks in Sri Lanka in 2019, in which a group of suicide bombers killed more than 260 civilians across three churches and hotels, is a case in point (Slater and Pereira 2019). Additionally, the Taliban's rule and its aftermath in Afghanistan and in the bordering North West Frontier Province (NWFP) of Pakistan have had grave ramifications for freedom of religion, especially in relation to women's equality rights.

In India, anti-minority rhetoric and violence, particularly targeted at Christians and Muslims, are perpetuated by Hindu nationalists who seek to make India a Hindu state (Mandalaparthy 2018). This activity is mirrored in Sri Lanka and Myanmar by Buddhist nationalism (Beech 2019). In 2018, the UN Special Rapporteur on Freedom of Religion, Belief or Conscience, Ahmed Shaheed, noted the disturbing trend of routine violations of freedom of religion in Asia, and he specifically referred to the discrimination faced by Christians in Pakistan and the military-led persecution faced by Christians and Muslims in Myanmar.[2]

All South Asian countries are steeped in patriarchy, manifested through the institutions of government, community, family and the market. Preference for sons over daughters and the low value accorded to female children has resulted in a low ratio of girls to boys in the region. One form of women's subordination that is prevalent across the region, irrespective of caste, class, religious, regional, linguistic and cultural disparities, is violence against women. Fuelled by misogyny, violence against women is also intimately connected with the growing power of politico-religious parties across the region (see Chhachhi 1991).

3. The status of women in minority religious communities

Although freedom of religion or belief (FoRB) has a universal application and rests on a rich, detailed human rights framework that is binding upon all states – including those in South Asia – its impact on women is disparate, in both majority and minority communities and in any given context. The superiority felt by a majority religious community in a particular country or region can trigger a sense of insecurity, threats of erosion of identity, and a sense of secondary citizenship within minority religious communities. Resistance to this pressure, in the form of assertion of identity, tends towards religious

---

[2] Shaheed spoke these words at the Fourth South East Asia Freedom of Religion or Belief conference, Bangkok, Thailand, August 2018.

conservatism within minority communities, with additional ramifications for women's equality rights. For example, in India, the Muslim minority resists reform of laws governing family relationships; in contrast, the family laws applicable to the Hindu community have witnessed far more reforms in the past seven decades since India's independence (see Joshi 2013). On the other hand, the reverse is true in Bangladesh, which has a Muslim majority and a Hindu minority community. Discriminatory provisions in family laws applicable to the Hindu community have been reformed more slowly than those applicable to Muslims in Bangladesh. For example, the existing Hindu law in Bangladesh prohibits inter-caste marriages, permits polygamy by the husband, does not allow dissolution of marriage (since it considers marriage to be a sacrament), does not require registration of marriages, and has far more discriminatory provisions on inheritance and succession rights of women than does Hindu law in India, which also discriminates against women to some extent (see Alam 2004). The precarious position of women in both India and Bangladesh indicates the multiple forms of discrimination they face due to the interplay of gender and religious identity.

The status of Muslim minority women remains in jeopardy in South Asia at this time. A case in point is the emergency regulation issued by the Sri Lankan government on 29 April 2019, prohibiting clothing that conceals the face, purportedly for security reasons. The prohibition adversely affects Muslim women, who must deal with both patriarchal forces within their community that insist on the face veil and state forces that prohibit it. The prohibition not only stigmatizes Muslim women, restricting their mobility and access to places of work, study and public services; it also violates their basic right to choose to dress in accordance with their religious beliefs (Amnesty International 2019). The regulation was promulgated in the wake of the April 2019 terror attacks on three churches in Sri Lanka.

4. Women's autonomy and agency

Most religions require women to be submissive to their husbands, fathers and sons. Fathers and husbands are often treated as guardians of the woman, in laws and in local customary practices. This leads to a denial of women's agency and autonomy in crucial decisions. The religious tradition of the father or brother 'giving the bride away' in marriage, which prevails in both Christian and Hindu communities, is a case in point. The Hindu religious tradition consists of a marriage ritual called *kanyadaan* (literally translated as gift of a virgin girl) when the bride is given to the bridegroom by her father or, in his absence, by her brother or another male member of her family. In the contemporary context, this might be nothing more than a symbolic act. However, it connotes a deeper message: the transfer of dominance over the woman from the father or brother to the husband, thereby undermining her personhood, personal autonomy and agency.

The case of Hadiya, a woman in India, illustrates the undermining of women's right to choose their religious faith or a partner belonging to a religion different from that of their parents. Hadiya, a 24-year-old student – originally Hindu and known by the name of Akhila – converted to Islam in 2016 and married Shafin, a Muslim man, several months later. Her father filed a writ petition in the Kerala High Court in India, alleging that she was forcibly converted and that her husband was a terrorist likely to take her to Syria to be recruited by the Islamic State. In response, the Kerala High Court annulled Hadiya's marriage to Shafin and placed her in her parents' custody, claiming that it was for her protection. It observed that "a girl aged 24 is weak and vulnerable, capable of being exploited in many ways."

Subsequently, Shafin, petitioned the Supreme Court of India, which, in its interim order, directed an investigation by the National Investigation Authority (NIA), a prime governmental body responsible for the investigation of anti-terror cases. In October 2018, the NIA concluded that there was no evidence of coercion or larger criminal design. The Supreme Court of India thereafter reversed the Kerala High Court's judgement and observed that the court's support for the parents of an adult daughter was "a manifestation of the idea of patriarchal autocracy and possibly self-obsession with the feeling that a female is a chattel."[3]

Although the Supreme Court's final judgement brought relief from the couple's victimization, some crucial questions remain unanswered. If Hadiya had been a 24-year-old Hindu man, who had converted to Islam and married a Muslim woman of his choice, would the Supreme Court have required an investigation by the NIA? Hadiya's statement that she exercised her own free will in this regard, without any duress, was not considered adequate by the Supreme Court. Until very late in the litigation process, the court showed no inclination to interact directly with her, postponing an opportunity for her to present her case and prolonging her house arrest at her parents' home. The social, cultural and political milieu played a contributory role in the infantilization and erasure of Hadiya's personhood that underlay the Supreme Court's direction to the NIA. This led to a restriction of her mobility and an extreme invasion of her privacy, and it exacerbated the violations of her fundamental rights.

5. Honour Crimes and Moral Policing

Honour crimes, which are widely prevalent in South Asian countries, offer further evidence of the sharp confluence between religious orthodoxy and fundamentalism, on one hand, and patriarchal forces that operate in the spheres of the family, community, market and state. Many such honour crimes, including rapes, gang

---

[3] Shafin Jahan vs. Asokan, K.M. 2018 SCC Online SC 343.

rapes, maiming and killing, have been triggered by inter-caste and inter-religious marriages and by the exercise of women's agency, which is seen as a transgression of the religious and social dictates of community leaders. *Khap panchayats* in India, *jirgas* in Pakistan, *shuras* in Afghanistan and *shalish* in Bangladesh are informal, male-centric, village-based systems that wield tremendous power over their communities and are often instrumental or complicit in such forms of sexual and gender-based violence. They perpetuate deeply patriarchal and fundamentalist norms regarding women, often deriving authority through religious and cultural norms, though they were established purportedly to administer justice. A detailed survey and discussion of various non-judicial systems in South Asia and their implications for women's rights have been undertaken elsewhere (see Ali et al 2017).

In a series of judgements, the Supreme Court of India strongly denounced the role of *khap panchayats* and other forms of kangaroo courts in violating women's human rights.[4] Courts in Bangladesh have further clarified that all alternative dispute resolution mechanisms such as conciliation and mediation, *shalish*, or traditional dispute resolution mechanisms for family disputes can be undertaken strictly within a legal framework, and punishment can be prescribed only as under the law, excluding the application of "any version of shari'a."[5] Similarly, the Supreme Court of Pakistan held that the system of *jirgas* and *panchayats*, inasmuch as they directed violence against women, violated Pakistan's international commitments under the International Covenant on Civil and Political Rights (ICCPR), the International Covenant on Economic, Social and Cultural Rights (ICESCR) and the Convention on Elimination of Discrimination Against Women (CEDAW).[6] Unfortunately, such progressive judgments are not effectively implemented at the ground level, and as a result such adjudicatory mechanisms continue to thrive.

6. Women in religious leadership

Women are often excluded from the hierarchies of religious power and either deterred from or rendered ineligible for religious office. As a result, in many religions, the priests and religious leaders are predominantly male. For example, there is no known history of a woman ever being the *shankaracharya* (head priest of

---

[4] Lata Singh v State of UP (2006) 5 SCC 475: (2006) 2 SCC (Cri) 478; Arumugam Seervai v State of Tamil Nadu (2011) 6 SCC 405: (2011) 2 SCC (Cri) 993; Shakti Vahini v Union of India (2018) 7 SCC 192.

[5] Bangladesh Legal Aid and Services Trust and Others vs. Government of Bangladesh and Others, order dated 8 July 2010 passed by Mr. Justice Syed Mahmud Hossain and Mr. Justice Gobinda Chandra Tagore in Writ Petition No.5863 of 2009 with Writ Petition No.754 of 2010 and Writ Petition No.4275 of 2010 (Bangladesh).

[6] National Commission on Status of Women and Another vs. Government of Pakistan and Others, judgement dated 16 January 2019 by Mr. Justice Mian Saqib Nisar and Mr. Justice Ijaz Ul Ahsan of the Supreme Court of Pakistan, in Constitution Petition No. 24 of 2012 and Civil Petition No. 773-P of 2018.

specific sects) in Hindu communities. The *ervad, mobed* and *dastur* (ranks of religious leaders in Zoroastrianism) and the *imams, qazis, mullahs* and *muftis* (religious leaders in Islam) have also been predominantly men. Although there has been a radical change in this arrangement within the Christian church in European countries in recent decades, the wave of reform has been slower within institutions in South Asian countries.

Hindu religious scriptures do not expressly disqualify women from becoming priests. However, in practice, most Hindu priests and spiritual mentors are men, due to their control of religious and spiritual knowledge. As observed by Santhanam and Yamunan (2015), this phenomenon has led to Hindu male priests exercising authority and hegemonic power. They have observed that the situation is similar amongst Muslim communities, where women are often excluded from addressing mixed congregations of men and women, issuing religious edicts or heading religious institutions such as the Wakf Boards.

To challenge male dominance in the religious sphere and to counter male hegemony, women have recently taken initiatives to pursue becoming *imams* (Muslim priests) or *pujaris* (Hindu priests). The judiciary has supported such initiatives from time to time. For example, in 2008 the Madras High Court in India allowed women to become priests in Hindu temples, with the observation that the altars of gods must be free from gender bias.[7] In Nepal, Hindu temples opened their doors to female priests in 2009. The temples were built by Dalits, who are considered untouchables and are lowest in the caste hierarchy ('Nepali Temples' 2009).

As a logical corollary of the exclusion of women from religious leadership, the power to interpret religious texts and beliefs has been consolidated by male religious leaders. Their teachings and interpretations have often been motivated by gender bias against women, perceived male superiority and the need to assume and maintain patriarchal control over essential matters at all stages of a woman's life, from cradle to grave. Women are denied the right to question such interpretations of religion. For example, in India, the traditional interpretations of the Qur'an with regard to polygamy and pronouncement of divorce have distinctly advocated and advanced male privilege. Feminist interpretations of the Qur'an are now being undertaken to neutralize and counter the effect of narrow, patriarchal and anti-female interpretations. Similarly, in Pakistan, progressive interpretations of the Qur'an are used to counter patriarchal state religion (Zia 2009:29). Indeed, the growth of Islamic feminism in much of South Asia is intrinsically linked to the urgent need felt for re-interpretation of religious texts and sources through the lens of feminism.

---

[7] Pinniyakkal vs. The District Collector, judgement delivered by Justice K. Chandru of the Madurai Bench of the Madras High Court, India, dated 1 September 2008.

7. Menstrual taboos and exclusionary practices

South Asia is also distinguished by its menstrual taboos and related exclusionary practices, particularly in Hindu communities. In the western parts of Nepal, the practice of *chhaupadi* still exists – a menstrual taboo under which women are banished from their homes during menstruation and prohibited from touching their family members, cattle, fruit-bearing plants or crops. This practice is founded on the belief that menstruating women are unclean and impure, and that therefore their touch can cause destruction. It draws its sanction from Hindu beliefs and customary practices, perpetuated by religious leaders with a patriarchal mindset. After the death of several women and their children in *chhaupadi* huts, and under local and global pressure from varied sources, in recent years the Supreme Court of Nepal and the Parliament have intervened to eliminate this practice by passing a judgement and legislation in this regard, respectively.[8]

Even though India and Nepal are neighbouring countries that share South Asian culture and traditions, and even though both have a Hindu-majority population, the menstrual taboos in the two countries have varied. In India, women have been historically denied access to certain places of public worship on the basis of notions of purity and pollution surrounding the natural, biological process of menstruation. For example, the Sabarimala is a famous Hindu hill temple situated in the southern state of Kerala and one of the most visited places of pilgrimage in the world. The deity in the temple is Lord Ayappa, who is believed to be eternally celibate. Women of menstrual age (10 to 50 years old) are prohibited from climbing the Sabari hills or entering the temple, on the ground that menstruation pollutes the temple, its deity and the male devotees. This prohibition has been enforced under rules formulated by the Kerala state government.[9] The Kerala High Court upheld the religious practice of prohibiting women of menstrual age from entering the temple. One of its reasons was that the exclusion has been practiced from time immemorial and hence does not violate the fundamental rights to equality and non-discrimination guaranteed under the Indian Constitution.[10] In 2018, the Supreme Court of India reversed this judgement and upheld women's fundamental right to equality, equal access to public places including temples, non-discrimination on grounds of sex and religion, and the application of freedom of religion equally to all women as well.[11] The Supreme Court's progressive

---

[8] Dil Bahadur Bishwokarma et al. v. HMG Office of Prime Minister and Council of Ministers et al., WPN 48, decided on 5 April 2005 by the Supreme Court of Nepal; Criminal Code Bill passed by the Parliament of Nepal on 9 August 2017.

[9] Rule 3(b) of the Kerala Hindu Places of Public Worship (Authorization of Entry) Rules, 1965.

[10] S. Mahendran v. The Secretary, Travancore Devaswom Board, AIR 1993 Ker 42.

[11] Indian Young Lawyers Association and Others v. the State of Kerala and Others *(2018) SCC Online SCC 1690.*

judgement drove home the point that religious beliefs should not be used to discriminate against women. However, implementation of the judgement has been difficult, since many view it as an unwarranted interference in the religious beliefs and practices of Hindus. Interestingly, the issue polarized the Hindu community, particularly the women – some of whom started a "happy to bleed" campaign in support of entry into the temple while others countered with a "ready to wait" campaign, in the name of respecting religious beliefs of male devotees to the temple (see Paul 2018).

8. Anti-conversion and blasphemy laws

Anti-conversion laws in India, Nepal and Sri Lanka have also resulted in grave violations of the exercise of freedom of religion. Anti-conversion laws criminalize 'improper' conversions, by treating them as forceful, fraudulent or coercive acts, or as effected through allurement or inducement (see Hertzberg 2020:93). The denial of women's agency in religious conversions and the gendered construction of women as gullible, helpless victims in such cases is not new. In India, several state-level anti-conversion laws provide for enhanced punishment if women are found to have been forcibly converted, based on a paternalistic and protective approach to women that negates their agency. For example, under S. 4 of the Orissa Freedom of Religion Act (OFRA, 1967), conversions of women, along with other categories of persons, found to be a result of "force," "fraud" or "inducement" (all of which are vaguely and broadly defined) can lead to imprisonment for up to two years (as opposed to one year for others) and a fine of up to Rs. 10,000 (as against Rs. 5000 for others). Other state legislations contain similar provisions. Such provisions have not been subjected to an equality challenge under the Indian Constitution and hence have been normalized within the Indian legal framework.

The blasphemy laws in operation in countries such as Pakistan may appear gender-neutral, but they have ominous and potent ramifications for women, with threats and risks of sexual and gender-based violence at the hands of self-appointed guardians of religion, in addition to death or excommunication. For example, Asiya Bibi – who was convicted of blasphemy and sentenced to death by a Pakistan court in 2010 and subsequently acquitted by the Supreme Court – was kept in protective custody to avert impending attacks on her, including possible sexual violence.[12]

9. The relevance of a human rights framework

As the preceding discussion illustrates, there is an overlap between FoRB and women's equality rights; however, Article 30 of the Universal Declaration of Human

---

[12] Mst. Asia Bibi v. the State etc., judgement of the Supreme Court of Pakistan delivered by Chief Justice Mian Saqib Nisar, Justice Asif Saeed Khan Khosa and Mr. Justice Mazhar Alam Khan Miankhel, 8 October 2018, in Criminal Appeal No. 39-L of 2015 against the judgement of the Lahore High Court dated 16 October 2014 in Crl.A.No.2509/2010 and M.R.No.614/2010.

Rights and Article 5 of the ICCPR expressly state that one human right cannot be used to extinguish or violate another human right. CEDAW calls upon States Parties to respect, protect and fulfil the human rights of women and to eliminate various forms of discrimination against women, both *de jure* (in law) and *de facto* (in practice). Articles 2(f) and 5(a) of CEDAW impose a positive obligation on States Parties to modify or abolish social and cultural practices and customs that discriminate against women. With the understanding that culture is a macro-concept, and with 'cultural practices' undergirding the religious norms of societies, the state obligation to modify discriminatory cultural practices (as declared in CEDAW) patently includes religious practices and beliefs. Moreover, the human-rights standards establish that FoRB is a right for all persons – including women – and hence women's right to FoRB must not be curtailed on the ground of religious beliefs or cultural practices. Furthermore, States are obliged to ensure that "traditional, historical, religious or cultural attitudes are not used to justify violations of women's right to equality."[13]

In 2010, the UN Special Rapporteur for FoRB at that time, Asma Jahangir, highlighted the discriminatory practices to which women were subjected, often in the name of religion or within their religious communities.[14] She suggested that women's rights should be prioritized over gender-based discrimination that was premised upon religious intolerance. In 2013, the lacuna left by the absence of a specific mention on freedom of religion and women's equality rights in any Convention or Declaration was addressed by the new UN Special Rapporteur on Freedom of Religion or Belief, Ahmed Shaheed, who prepared and presented a report on the relationship between the two human rights of FoRB and gender equality.[15] Acknowledging the complex problems that exist at this intersection, the Special Rapporteur observed that measures to address religious discrimination may follow a male understanding of the needs and requirements of society, whereas programmes that focus on eliminating discrimination against women may lack sensitivity in matters of religious diversity.[16] The report also reiterated the need to explore and create synergies between the two, observing:

> [T]he abstractly antagonistic misconstruction of the relationship between freedom of religion or belief and equality between men and women fails to do justice to the

---

[13] General Comment 28 on Article 3 of the ICCPR, 2000 (equality of rights between men and women); adopted at the sixty-eighth session of the Human Rights Committee, 29 March 2000, CCPR/C/21/Rev.1/Add.10, para 5.

[14] A/65/207, para 69.

[15] A/68/290, 7 August 2013.

[16] Ibid, para 18.

life situation of many millions of individuals whose specific needs, wishes, claims, experiences and vulnerabilities fall into the intersection of both human rights, a problem disproportionately affecting women from religious minorities.[17]

In March 2020, the UN Special Rapporteur on FoRB further clarified that states should not use religious beliefs to justify violence or discrimination against women, and that freedom of religion protects individuals and not religions as such.[18]

In addition, the UN Special Rapporteur, in a report on the elimination of all forms of religious intolerance, also called for a "global repeal of blasphemy laws" and emphasized that anti-conversion laws, anti-apostasy laws and blasphemy laws ... often serve as platforms for enabling incitement to discrimination, hostility or violence against persons based on religion or belief.[19]

South Asian states have ratified most of the major human-rights conventions including the ICCPR, ICESCR and CEDAW. They are duty-bound to adhere to the normative standards created by such conventions, as well as reports and recommendations of UN Special Rapporteurs, independent experts, working groups and other special-procedure mechanisms. Such standards include states' responsibility to respect, protect and fulfil women's human rights. The UN Special Rapporteurs' reports that proscribe violence and discrimination against women in the name of religion are as relevant to South Asian countries as to other regions of the world. The reports draw upon consultations with a range of actors – state and non-state – across the world, including from the South Asian region. Granted, some distinctly South Asian religious beliefs, practices, socio-political contexts and challenges may not be specifically captured or echoed in the UN reports. However, civil-society actors and women's movements in each country can use the international standards as a yardstick, contextualizing and applying them to make their governments responsive and vigilant in preventing violations and in providing redress should a violation take place.

Arguments, based on cultural relativism, that reject universal human rights and justify violence and discrimination against women on the basis of specific religious beliefs and cultural practices unique to the South Asian region are problematic. Equally troublesome are arguments based on cultural essentialism, which views some religions and cultures as inherently misogynist, violent, or discriminatory against women. Religious fundamentalism and patriarchy are all-pervasive. Although the needed solutions must address discriminatory practices and violence

---

[17] Ibid, para 68.
[18] A/HRC/43/48, 27 February 2020.
[19] A/72/365, 28 August 2017, para 27.

against women at the ground level, international human-rights standards can play an important role in facilitating this development.

10. Towards a collaborative project of FoRB and women's equality rights

FoRB and women's equality rights are intrinsically linked and mutually reinforce each other. Absence of FoRB for women is an obstacle to gender equality. Very often, violations of women's rights are inter-linked with a denial of women's right to choose for themselves what they believe in and how they wish to live their lives on the basis of those beliefs. Therefore, it is vital to integrate FoRB for all and women's rights agendas if we are to achieve results in either realm.

FoRB is equally a freedom for women as for men, and equally for women from minority and majority communities. We need to acknowledge that women have the right to enjoy FoRB independent of any man; often women are seen as passive practitioners and recipients of religion, whereas men are seen as active agents and interpreters of religion. This situation cries out for change.

In the South Asian context, where politics and religion are closely fused and where women face an onslaught on their human rights in the name of religious beliefs and customary practices on a regular basis, it is important to explore how synergies between freedom of religion and women's rights can be fostered. We need a dialogue between religious and secular leadership, as well as with women's rights groups, that recognizes the fact that religion plays a significant role in many women's lives, but also that religious beliefs, texts and teachings can serve as roadblocks as well as resources with regard to the empowerment of women. At the same time, governments have a crucial role in ensuring that such a process of dialogue is not adversely affected or scuttled by religious fundamentalist and patriarchal forces in furtherance of their vested interests. Deepening the critical examination of religious texts, beliefs and practices and exploring new interpretations that harmonize women's rights with freedom of religion are vital, so that the roadblocks may be minimized and the resources maximized.

References

Alam, M. Shah. 2004. 'Review of Hindu Personal Law in Bangladesh: Search for Reforms', *Bangladesh Journal of Law*, 8(1-2), pp. 15-52.

Ali, Feroze, Mathew SK, Gopalaswamy AK and Babu MS. 2017. *Systematic Review of Different Models and Approaches of Non-State Justice Systems in South Asia and Its Complementarity with the State Justice Delivery Systems*. London: EPPI-Centre, Social Science Research Unit, UCL Institute of Education, University College London.

Amnesty International. 2019. *Sri Lanka: Ban on Face Veil Risks Stigmatizing Muslim Women*, [online]. Available at: https://www.amnesty.org/en/latest/news/2019/04/sri-lanka-ban-on-face-veil-risks-stigmatizing-muslim-women/.

Beech, Hannah. 2019. 'Buddhists Go to Battle: When Nationalism Overrides Pacifism', *New York Times*, [online]. Available at: https://t.co/ynVXHC57cc.

Engels, Friederick. 1966. 'Bruno Bauer and Early Christianity' in Marx, Karl and Friederick Engels *On Religion*. Moscow: Progress Publishers, pp. 194-204.

Chatterji, Jyotsana. n.d. *Changes in Christian Personal Laws: A Brief Account of the Advocacy Process*, [online]. Available at: https://feministlawarchives.pldindia.org/wp-content/uploads/19.pdf.

Chhachhi, Amrita. 1991. 'The State, Religious Fundamentalism and Women in South Asia' in Nijeholt, Geertje (ed.) *Towards Women's Strategies in the 1990s: Challenging Government and the State*. London: Palgrave Macmillan, pp. 16-50.

Dhume, Sadanand. 2019. 'South Asia is Islamic State's New Target', *Wall Street Journal*. Available at: https://www.wsj.com/articles/south-asia-is-islamic-states-new-target-11556837481.

Engineer, Asghar Ali. 1975. 'Origin and Development of Islam', *Social Scientist* 3(9), pp. 22-44.

Haslegrave, Marianne. 2004. 'Implementing the ICPD Programme of Action: What a Difference a Decade Makes', *Reproductive Health Matters* 12(23), pp. 12-18.

Hertzberg, Michael. 2020. 'The Gifts of Allurement: Anti-Conversion Legislation, Gift-giving and Political Allegiance in South Asia', *Journal of Contemporary Religion* 35(1), pp. 93-114.

Idara, Inna Reddy. 2017. 'Religion Is a Subset of Culture and an Expression of Spirituality', *Advances in Anthropology* 7, pp. 273-88.

Joshi, Divij. 2013. 'Family Law Reforms in India: Historical and Judicial Perspectives, [online]. Available at: https://ssrn.com/abstract=2200165 or http://dx.doi.org/10.2139/ssrn.2200165.

Khan, Borhan Uddin and Muhammad Mahbubur Rahman. 2009. 'Freedom of Religion in South Asia: Implications for Minorities', *European Yearbook of Minority Issues*, 8, pp. 367-86.

Mandalaparthy, Nikhil. 2018. 'Rising Hindu Nationalism in South Asia: Implications for the United States', *The Diplomat*, [online]. Available at: https://bit.ly/2SDHrDK.

'Nepali Temples Open Doors to Women Priests.' 2009. *The Star*, [online]. Available at: https://bit.ly/3jIM635.

Paul, Cithara. 2018. 'When Sabarimala Entry Issue Spawned "Happy to Bleed," "Ready to Wait"' *The Week*, [online]. Available at: https://bit.ly/3OLudsU.

Puri, Harish K. 2003. 'Scheduled Castes in Sikh Community: A Historical Perspective', *Economic and Political Weekly* 38(26), pp. 2693-2701.

Santhanam, Radhika and Sruthisagar Yamunan. 2015. 'Wife, Mother, Lawyer, Priest', *The Hindu*, [online]. Available at: https://www.thehindu.com/opinion/op-ed/wife-mother-lawyer-priest/article7522954.ece.

Slater, Joanna Slater and Amantha Perera. 2019. 'At Least 290 Killed in Easter Sunday Attacks on Churches and Hotels', *Washington Post*. Available at: https://wapo.st/3jU1xoU.

Steffanus Alliance International. 2017. *Freedom of Religion or Belief for Everyone*. 4th edn. Oslo: Steffanus Alliance International.

Yilmaz, Muzaffer Ercan. 2006. 'Religious Fundamentalism and Conflict', *International Journal of Human Sciences*, 2(2).

Zia, Afiya Shehrbano. 2009. 'The Reinvention of Feminism in Pakistan', *Feminist Review*, 91, pp. 29-46.

Strengthening resilience among women from Christian minorities

The Strength2Stand approach

Rachel[1]

Abstract

This paper considers how the "Strength2Stand" approach can build the resilience of women belonging to Christian minorities. Following a brief overview of resilience based on research in different sectors in international development, it looks at the compound vulnerability of Christian women. Empirical evidence shows the success of the "Strength2Stand" approach. This approach is based on a three-tier pyramid of self-help development steps that are community-based and community-driven. Women can gradually improve their condition and position within their family and community, integrating spiritual, social and economic development in the process of empowerment and resilience building.

Keywords Resilience, compound vulnerability, religious minority, women, Strength2Stand approach.

1. Introduction

Pew Forum research has indicated a recent increase in restrictions on religion. In the last ten years, the number of governments imposing restrictions on religious minorities have risen from 40 to 52. The number of countries where people are experiencing the highest levels of social hostility due to religious diversity has grown from 39 to 56. This trend calls for a focus on strengthening Christian resilience to deal with the growing religious restrictions and social threats.

This paper captures my observations as a development practitioner among Christian minorities. I begin with some general observations on resilience, followed by a presentation of resilience models. I then discuss the problem of compound

---

[1] Rachel (a pseudonym) has been involved in community development for over 25 years. She is an expert in grass-roots community development in a variety of volatile and unpredictable contexts such as Afghanistan, Pakistan, Sudan, Iran and Egypt. Rachel's work focuses on empowerment of the most vulnerable, gender mainstreaming, facilitation of change processes and training in results-based monitoring. She works with Christian minorities on ways to strengthen resilience and general living conditions. Article submitted: 22 July 2019, accepted: 25 May 2020. The author can be contacted via the managing editor.

vulnerability for women,[2] taking into account the intersectionality[3] between their position as Christians in their family, as members of a religious minority and (in many cases) as living in poverty. The second section of the paper gives an overview of communal and cultural factors that prevent women from taking the initiative to promote their own development. The third section describes a community development model through which different aspects of the compound vulnerability are addressed, followed by some concluding thoughts.

1.1 Resilience in women belonging to a minority

In my experience, Christian minorities have generally seemed to be inward-looking, lacking positive resilience and strength to deal with the day-to-day challenges they face as a religious minority. This mindset causes them to see themselves as victims and to lose the ability to proactively mitigate negative consequences of pressure and discrimination. This observation triggered my interest in the concept of resilience, as well as my desire to find a model that I could apply to assist Christian minorities, particularly Christian women.

In general, Christian minority women live in a social circle limited to family and church. From childhood onwards, they are told to endure daily pressures and not challenge them, since they are supposed to live as devout, submissive female Christians. This endurance could actually be seen as a form of resilience, helping them cope with daily pressures. However, the pressure to live as submissive women often reduces women's space to develop new capacities outside the routines of daily life. There is no space in their social-relational and emotional realms to gain additional skills or explore new venues in study and employment; hence, no strengthening of resilience occurs. This article looks at one way to build the resilience of Christian women.

1.2 Some examples of a resilient system

The term 'resilience' has become a buzzword in the world of international development and has been used much more often during the last decade. The Overseas Development Institute (ODI) resilience scan[4] describes the focus on resilience that

---

[2] This term is borrowed from Emma Dipper, member of the Gender and Persecution Working group in the International Platform for Religious Freedom. Compound vulnerability is a situation in which systemic or institutional conditions intersect in a manner that creates additional barriers to the agent's ability to develop or achieve well-being, thus adding to the first-order vulnerability.

[3] Intersectionality is a theoretical framework for understanding how aspects of a person's social and political identities (e.g. gender, sex, race, class, sexuality, religion, ability, physical appearance, height) might combine to create unique modes of discrimination and privilege.

[4] Amy Kerbyshire et al., Resilience Scan, July–September 2017 (London: Overseas Development Institute, 2017) Available at: https://www.odi.org/sites/odi.org.uk/files/resource-documents/11966.

is present in many sectors within the arena of international development, as communities are supported to deal with vulnerabilities such as during recovery after natural disasters, peacebuilding and mediation after civil war, and dealing with persistent poverty.

The ODI has defined resilience as the "ability to anticipate, avoid, plan for, cope with, recover from and adapt to shocks and stresses."[5] This means that people can deal with changing circumstances, proactively making the best of each situation they are in. They can bounce back after incidents of discrimination, taking steps to deal with changing realities.

The Resilience Alliance (an international, multidisciplinary research organization that explores the dynamics of human systems) has advanced the understanding and practical application of resilience, bringing in adaptive capacity, and transformation of societies and ecosystems to cope with change and support human well-being. It contends that systems can achieve resilience only within given limits; it represents the amount of change a system can undergo and still retain the same controls of function and structure, including the degree to which a system is capable of self-organization and able to establish or increase its capacity for learning and adaptation. In this view, once a certain threshold has been reached, transformation is needed to obtain a new state of resilience. The notion of moving beyond a threshold is a necessary component in thinking about well-being with regard to change, which could also be called *transformational change* as the goal is for the change to become adopted, sustained and integrated in life. Individual resilience is strongest when integrated with resilience building at the level of an organization, such as a church.

Another model developed to address the lack of resilience is the triple A+T model, developed by Building Resilience and Adaptation to Climate Extremes and Disasters (BRACED) and the UK Department for International Development (DFID), which administers British overseas aid.[6] The first A stands for *anticipate*: train the community

---

pdf, esp. 9. And ODI, "A comparative overview of resilience measurement frameworks". Available at: https://www.odi.org/sites/odi.org.uk/files/odi-assets/publications-opinion-files/9754.pdf.

[5] Building Resilience and Adaptation to Climate Extremes and Disasters (BRACED) developed the following definition: "If the capacities and assets to deal with various shocks, stresses, uncertainty and change are built and supported, and if drivers of risk are reduced, and if these actions are supported by an enabling environment, then resilience is increased." See Julia Barrott, "The 3As: Tracking Resilience across BRACED". Available at: https://www.weadapt.org/knowledge-base/transforming-development-and-disaster-risk/the-3as-tracking-resilience. The Organisation for Economic Co-operation and Development has defined resilience as "the ability of households, communities and nations to absorb and recover from shocks, whilst positively adapting and transforming their structures and means for living in the face of long-term stresses, change and uncertainty"; OECD, "Guidelines for Resilience Systems Analysis". Available at: http://www.oecd.org/dac/conflict-fragility-resilience/risk-resilience/.

[6] braced.org/about/.

in how to anticipate potential natural hazards or other risks, such as oppression by dominant majority religions. The second A stands for *absorb* – i.e. absorbing shocks or potential changes to individuals or groups that lead to a new situation. The third A signifies that people gain skills and use resources in order to *adapt*. These steps of resilience building lead then to the T, *transformation*, as the community introduces positive changes to deal with the new reality on the ground and to continue from there. People can then bounce forward with an element of optimism, aiming to adopt positive behavior so as to deal more effectively with pressure and discrimination.[7]

The resilience paradigms described above were developed by international development practitioners looking at socio-ecological issues overall; they do not provide an in-depth exploration of resilience building for religious minorities specifically. This paper looks specifically at how the triple A+T and bouncing forward could be appropriated to help Christian women under strain to build their resilience.

1.3 Compound vulnerability for women

A specific focus on women is important because they often face compound vulnerability due to the combination or intersectionality of different factors. First, they face pressure as a result of belonging to a religious minority; second, they often experience inferior status as women within their own family and religious community; third, religious minorities tend to live in poverty, a situation perpetuated by a lack of livelihood options and fewer educational opportunities. All these components together shape the intersectionality framework.

Intersectionality conceptualizes a person, a group or a social problem as affected by a number of forms of discrimination and disadvantages. It takes into account people's overlapping identities and experiences to understand the complexity of prejudices they face. Christian women have different kinds of pressures in the different social circles they move in, such as the general community, their church and their own family, thereby creating compound vulnerability.

Certain vulnerabilities can develop and become intensified due to deeper social-relational patterns and identity issues in society. For example, in Pakistan, social norms perpetuate and magnify the view that women have significantly less value than men. As a result, women risk developing a mindset of worthlessness, leading to a strong, internalized sense of inferiority that grows over a lifetime. But in the same way, resilience can unfold over a lifetime and be strongly influenced by family relationships, such, as those with one's husband or mother-in-law.[8]

---

[7] Manyena, S. B. (2009). Disaster resilience in development and humanitarian interventions. University of Northumbria.

[8] See for instance: Muliha Gull Tara and Venkat Rao Pulla ‚2014.'Patriarchy, Gender Violence and Poverty amongst Pakistani Women: A Social Work Inquiry', Int'l Journal of Social Work and Human Services,

Christian women also belong to informal communities, most importantly their (extended) family and church. Many internal and external factors affect these systems: social relationships of power, economic development, cultural traits, customary law and spirituality. These aspects must be considered when one seeks to address women's lack of resilience. In addition, decisions to strengthen resilience depend on personal traits such as perceived urgency, risk perception, cognitive barriers and personal and cultural values. The factors mentioned above are linked together in the social-relational sphere and need to be taken into account during the ongoing endeavour to strengthen resilience.

2. The community impacts Christian women's ability to be resilient

In my work as an international development practitioner, I have often observed patterns of lack of resilience amongst Christian women at the grassroots level, as they feel overwhelmed by daily discrimination and social hostility. Their internalized sense of inferiority, lack of self-confidence, relegation to the lower rungs of the household hierarchy, and lack of knowledge regarding their rights and entitlements prevent them from taking initiative.

Following are some concrete examples of what I have observed within the Christian communities in Egypt, Pakistan and Iraq:

1. A rather strict hierarchy within religious institutions, which leads to an authority gap and barrier between the (usually male) religious authorities and women. This results in the loss of opportunities to develop confidence and leadership skills.
2. A general hesitancy and fear of change of the status quo by people in power: leaders either male or female in position would like to keep their position instead of sharing or delegating power leading to *a halt of* change initiatives.
3. A Pakistani colleague confirmed that she is being influenced by the majority religion. She has unconsciously integrated part of the majority religion's culture within her own attitudes and behaviours. This includes the submissive role of women, the custom to men enjoying their meal before the women, and a conservative dress code. The non-Christian influences are accepted, and steps to address their inroads in the Christian culture are not seen as important.
4. Individuals are caught in the customary system of the local culture where change is not welcomed. Girls and women are expected to be compliant and go with the flow, for it "always has been like this and it will always continue as it is." Individuals do not like to stand out from the crowd; for instance, girls are

not encouraged to start a micro-business, to be in charge of their own income-generating activity, or to pursue higher education.
5. Decisions are often limited by the decisions one has made in the past, or by their experience up to that date, even though circumstances might have changed and past experiences may no longer be relevant. For example, a family may have moved to a more secure environment, however their daughters still do not receive permission to attend school beyond grade 8, even though security cannot be given as reason anymore.
6. Families where sons and daughters-in-law live with parents are often in a situation where the younger generation is hesitant to change habits so as to not offend their parents. As a result, women are further restricted from taking initiative to change. As one colleague told me, "My mother-in-law passed away; I now have freedom."
7. The oppressed accept their position and even self-perpetuate it by developing false beliefs of blame with sentences such as: "I should not have been there," "Why did I take this job?" and so on.
8. This mindset and belief cause women to treat the oppression they face as an excuse not to take action to change their situation. They willingly, probably unconsciously, become victimized, explaining their passivity by saying, "I cannot do that, as I am a woman. I don't have a man speaking for me. How can I raise my voice?"
9. Lack of assertiveness and ability to say no, low self-confidence, and self-doubt.

These points illustrate a variety of factors that must be considered when we support Christian women in addressing their position or their condition of vulnerability. Most of the factors are internal. Many external factors are present as well, such as support for income-generating activities to raise Christians out of poverty of advocating for political inclusion. However, these external factors are beyond the scope of this paper.

3. A suggested approach: Strength2Stand groups

How, then, can Christian women develop resilience despite their compound vulnerabilities and the resistance they experience in their community? How can they anticipate, absorb and adapt in response to their daily pressures? One suggested approach is Strength2Stand (S2S), introduced in Pakistan and Egypt by the UK organization Release International beginning in 2014. It is a self-help approach with a three-tier structure through which people come to realize that they can help themselves to achieve the economic, social and leadership goals they define.

The first tier in S2S is the presence of women's groups where the focus is on personal and family development. At the second tier, representatives of these S2S groups form an association, which focuses on changes within their own community. The third tier is formed by representatives of these associations, who come together to advocate for changes in the position of Christian women.

The main pillars of S2S are that (1) everyone is created in the image of God, and therefore we are all unique and worthy; (2) we all are created with different gifts and capacities; and (3) together we are strong; it is possible to create demand-making power through coordination and cooperation.

The S2S group functions as a place where women develop the skills and discipline necessary to conduct a meeting, collect savings, guide a discussion. In addition, as a safe space, they reflect on family relationships, learn about responsibility and accountability and care for each other. The most vulnerable are selected through criteria set by church leaders and/or community members themselves. Weekly meetings of 15 to 20 women living in the same neighborhood strengthen social cohesion. An external facilitator focuses on capacity building according to a curriculum through which the S2S group members learn to focus on spiritual growth, economic development and a process of empowerment. They also learn how to address cases of discrimination and oppression.

All group meetings start with devotions, prayer and a discussion of how to apply the biblical message in daily life. Group members take turns leading the devotions, thus building the capacity to read the Bible and to guide a basic discussion on the content of the reading. These skills assist the members to look at their own situation, discussing how they can adapt in order to mitigate harmful conditions. For instance, a devotion on Abigail's actions to avoid David's wrath conveys the message that women should step up to stop harmful events if needed, just as Abigail anticipated how David would respond and acted accordingly.

The meetings continue with discussion of social issues. Ideally, the topic of the devotion is linked to the social issue under consideration, such as relationships with spouses, parents and children, education, literacy or health issues. Members learn how to adapt so as to avoid harmful situations – for example, to avoid certain inflammatory words such as 'equality,' as many men in their families do not accept women as equal partners. Women stress the importance of respect, following the example of Jesus' respect for women.

As Christian women commonly face compound vulnerability, this approach aims to address different aspects of vulnerability, including economic poverty. Empirical evidence from Sudan, Pakistan and Egypt shows that S2S helps Christian women learn to take the initiative to support each other, to start income-generating activity and to advise each other on how to deal with tension within family relationships. Playing a role in efforts to make ends meet for the family enhances self-confidence and decreases the strong, internalized sense of inferiority.

Once the S2S group has developed the capacity to function on its own, the external facilitator transitions out and members lead the groups themselves. At this point (the programme's second tier) representatives are selected to lead an association. Within the association, members discuss ways to anticipate daily pressures and how to adapt to them so as to protect their own dignity and that of their loved ones in the community. Representatives focus on strategies to strengthen the process of empowerment for S2S group members.

At this level of operation, S2S members in Sudan claimed a decision-making role within the church. In Egypt, S2S members claimed physical space within the church as a meeting location. Stronger S2S groups requested the priest to facilitate group meetings for their husbands and brothers to enable a process where the men could also discuss issues important for them.

This process becomes still stronger at the third level, called the federation, where members learn how to lobby and advocate to transform the mindset of society (external factors). At the third tier, members are equipped to play a significant role in producing systemic change – perhaps examining aspects of prejudice in the educational system, promoting gender equality, addressing unequal power relationships within the family and church, or facilitating a process by which religious leaders include women in decision-making processes. The goal is to establish an enabling environment where women can develop their abilities, thrive and rejoice as daughters of God, created in His image. This level has not been reached yet within the communities where I have worked and observed S2S.

S2S is a good start towards building female church members' confidence, self-esteem and social cohesion so that they support each other in strengthening their capabilities.[9] This process alone, however, is insufficient by itself to cause sustainable change. Ideally, S2S should be complemented by other capacity-building initiatives to produce transformational change at both the individual and community levels. For instance, Pakistan is currently pioneering male S2S groups, for young men in the same villages and communities where female S2S groups are also meeting. The objective is to discuss similar topics in both groups, fostering a process of building dignified relationships between men and women and eventually leading to more equal gender relationships.

---

[9] See Sabina Alkire and Séverine Deneulin, 2009. 'The Human Development and Capability Approach' in Deneulin, Séverine and Lila Shahani (eds.) *An Introduction to the Human Development and Capability Approach*. London: Earthscan, pp. 22-48. The capability approach contains three central concepts: functioning, capability and agency. Functioning refers to being or doing what people value and have reason to value. A capability signifies a person's freedom to enjoy various functionings – to be or do things that contribute to their well-being. Agency is one's ability to pursue and realize goals he or she values and has reason to value. The capability approach is multi-dimensional, because several things matter at the same time. Well-being cannot be reduced to income, happiness or any other single thing.

Christian communities need to support each other and to develop protective mechanisms to protect their dignity and value, which could include very simple measures such as walking girls to school to prevent them from being harassed. In addition, they can develop a sense of discernment, learn to interpret their cultural situation, be proactive and discover new ways to strengthen their own community.

4. Conclusion and the way forward

How does one go forward in building resilience amongst minority Christian women and their communities? Christians and their communities must take multiple factors and development strategies into account when addressing women's lack of resilience. Women have a tremendous influence over their children, particularly in societies (like most of those I have visited) where they are seen as traditional caretakers. Strong, resilient Christian women serving as caretakers can guide and support their family members to deal with pressures in life. However, this is a long process that must be complemented by other initiatives.

The three-tier structure of Strength2Stand gradually builds women's capacity and skill to anticipate, absorb and adapt in the midst of pressures and discrimination. It has a strong focus on equipping women and girls to influence children and male family members. This mutually supportive social network in which Christian women share with and learn from each other is a valuable first step.

It is essential to strengthen the resilience of minority Christian groups as persecution is likely to increase in the foreseeable future. The S2S approach alone is insufficient in enabling minority women to realize their full worth. A comprehensive, systemic approach is needed for these women to truly move beyond becoming victims, and for the community at large to truly become resilient. People in positions of authority play a strong role in promoting inclusiveness and the acceptance of Christian women as precious children of God. Moving forward, further steps could involve the following:
➢ breaking down those elements in the power hierarchy that hinder development (including the church hierarchy);
➢ building the capacity to discern non-biblical influences in the church and Christian community;
➢ strengthening the self-esteem and confidence of women and girls, as well as marginalized male members; and
➢ developing skills to proactively protect oneself and other women and girls.

It is about time to build up resilience within Christian minorities!

IIRF Reports

A monthly journal with special reports,
research projects, reprints and documentation
published by the
International Institute for Religious Freedom
(Bonn – Cape Town – Colombo)

www.iirf.eu/iirfreports

Christian women facing persecution in India
A review and recommendations
Jayakumar Ramachandran[1]

Abstract

Christian women face many forms of discrimination in India, but India is also one of the world's most troublesome countries with regard to the treatment of women generally. It is thus important to distinguish, within the double persecution that women face, when they are suffering as Christians and when they are targeted simply for being women. This article gives examples of Christian women in India who have been persecuted exclusively for their faith, for both their faith and their gender, or not at all. It then explores identifiable causes of the persecution of Christians and offers suggestions as to how the church should respond.

Keywords Discrimination, violence, patriarchy, Hindu fundamentalism, freedom of religion, India.

1. Introduction

On the 2019 Open Doors World Watch List, which identifies the 50 countries where religious persecution is most severe, India ranked tenth (Open Doors 2019). Targeted violence and hate crimes against the Christian community in India have continued unabated. The Religious Liberty Commission of the Evangelical Fellowship of India recorded 325 incidents in 2018 where Christians were targeted with violence, intimidation or harassment.

Religious persecution is a complex and diverse phenomenon (Sauer and Schirrmacher 2012:14). This paper looks at one component of it, namely the persecution of women. I first consider the difficulties experienced by Indian women in general before looking at cases involving Christian women. I then analyse the causes of such persecution and offer recommendations as to how to respond to it. One purpose of this paper is to determine whether Christian women's religious faith alone is the cause of persecution or if other factors are involved.

---

[1] Jayakumar Ramachandran (DMin, Columbia International University, USA) is the founder of Bible Believing Churches and Missions and General Secretary of the Indian Institute of Inter-Cultural Studies, Bangalore, India. He is currently doing post-doctoral work at the University of South Africa on mission in India and persecution of Christian converts. Article received: 15 May 2019; accepted: 14 May 2020. Email: jkbbcm@gmail.com.

2. Discrimination and violence against Indian women in general

Discrimination against women remains a major issue in India. A 2018 study by the Thomson Reuters Foundation named India the most dangerous country for women. India was top-ranked on three of the criteria: the risk of sexual violence and harassment against women; the dangers women face from cultural, tribal and traditional practices; and the risks of human trafficking including forced labour, sex slavery and domestic servitude (Goldsmith and Beresford 2018). It is further claimed that in the extremely patriarchal northern region of India, women are discriminated against within their own families (Bertelsmann Stiftung 2018).

Discrimination against women is prevalent everywhere in the world and more so in Indian society (R. Sharma 2015:141-42). Some particular types of discrimination are discussed below.

Sex selection: Discrimination begins at the pre-natal stage. The underlying cause for sex selection or 'son preference' is related to the difficulties involved in bearing daughters, which include significant social and economic costs (Priya et al 2014:18).

Gender-based violence: This problem is rooted in India's social, cultural and economic context (I. Sharma 2015:131-32). Central to this problem is the fact that Indian men and women have been trained to believe that men's dominance over women is normal and that acts of violence against women are justified. Forms of gender-based violence include psychological abuse, sexual harassment, sexual exploitation and abuse, intimate partner violence, and deprivation of education, food, economic and health resources. Of the 338,924 crimes committed against women in India during 2016, the most common categories were cruelty by husband or relatives (32.6%), assault on women with intent to violate her modesty (25.0%), kidnapping and abduction (19.0%), and rape (11.5%) (National Crime Records Bureau 2017).

Dowry disaster: The level of violence and killings linked to dowry payments is alarming. Data from the National Crime Records Bureau suggest an increase in crimes reported under the Dowry Prohibition Act since 2008, and a significant increase in such crimes and dowry-related deaths by 2012 (National Crime Records Bureau 2013:81). One researcher claimed that 22 women per day were killed in dowry-related murders in India (Storkey 2015:79). In 2015 alone, 1,781 women reportedly committed dowry-related suicides (National Crime Records Bureau 2016:201).

Exploitation of patriarchal culture: According to the *Laws of Manu* (a sacred Hindu text),[2] "In childhood a female must be subject to her father, in youth to her

---

[2] I have used the translation of the Laws of Manu available at https://bit.ly/3ekumZN.

husband, when her lord is dead to her sons; a woman must never be independent." This is still the case in the modern-day social structure.

2.1 Discrimination and violence against female Christian converts in India

Christian women are not spared from the above-mentioned atrocities. In many cases, they experience double persecution for being both Christians and women. To what extent does being Christian influence the discrimination and violence? To help in answering that question, I classify victims into three categories: doubly afflicted female victims, unafflicted Christian women, and women clearly afflicted due to their faith.

2.1.1 Doubly afflicted female Christian converts

Communal violence in India disproportionately affects India's religious minorities – especially Muslims, but also Christians and Sikhs. While often instrumentalized for political gains, communal violence draws on and exacerbates a climate of entrenched discrimination against India's religious minorities, with far-reaching social, economic, cultural and political dimensions. Such violence is frequently committed with impunity and sometimes even with the direct complicity of state actors, which ranges from inciting violence through hate speech to refusing to properly investigate communal incidents after they have occurred (Center for Study of Society and Secularism and Minority Rights Group International 2017:3).

An account by Cyrilla Chakkalakal, a Franciscan Sister of St. Mary of the Holy Angels, is helpful. She outlined her experiences of pain in the lives of nuns arising from patriarchal attitudes at a nationwide consultation (Saldanha 2016). Referring to the murder of two sisters from her congregation in 1990, she narrated how the character assassination of the sisters in the media turned public attention to their sexuality and away from the crimes committed. The leaders of the Catholic community failed to take a stand. Their apathy and silence were painful.

Religious structures can have a negative impact on victims of sexual abuse too. Females internalize scriptural interpretations that describe women stereotypically as sinner, manipulator and temptress. This contributes to their silence when dealing with abuse. Seeing the priest as in the place of God compounds the confusion and guilt. As a result, the psycho-social and spiritual impact of abuse committed by the clergy can be immense.

The bodies of women from the Dalit or outcast community are seen as 'available,' and these women are portrayed as characterless, causing them to be exploited for sex. Atrocities against Dalit women are very visible and committed with utter impunity. The internalization of their social status renders them voiceless. The mindset of caste underpins culture in all religious groups, including Christians (Saldanha 2016).

2.1.2 Unafflicted female Christian converts

On the other hand, many female Christians in India, some of them quite prominent, have faced little or no difficulty after becoming Christians. For example, Mohini, an actress (the pseudonym of Mahalakshmi), a Brahmin born in Tanjore, Tamil Nadu, became a Christian and took on the name of Christeena, without facing any social pressures (Song on Fire 2016).

Pandita Ramabai, a prominent Christian convert, experienced hardships, but not on account of her faith; it was more caste-related. Since she was a high-caste Brahmin, her marriage to Bipin Bihari Medhavi, an untouchable, was unacceptable in the society she lived in. She accepted Christ while in England in 1889 (Jayawardena 1995:54). On her return to India, she established outstanding mission work amongst widows and the destitute (Frykenberg 2016:67). This committed Indian Christian female convert of strong character, so bold in her compassion, and with a dazzling capacity to organize relief work with selfless service and dedication, did not face pressure due to her faith.

Sister Nirmala Joshi, who succeeded Nobel laureate Mother Teresa as head of the Missionaries of Charity, was born in a Nepali Brahmin family but eventually converted to Catholicism. India's government bestowed on her the Padma Vibhushan, the second-highest award granted to civilians, on 26 January 2009 for her service to the nation. Sister Nirmala did not face any pressure resulting from her conversion (Pandya 2015).

An actress named Pusbalatha, originally Catholic, became a practicing Hindu and later married A. V. M. Rajan, an actor who had been born Hindu. She also experienced no pressure due to her conversion (Robinson 2013).

Anju Panta, of Nepali Hindu origin, is a very prominent *ghazal* and playback singer. After her conversion to Christianity, she refused to perform at a Hindu festival, saying that her faith in the true God did not allow her to worship other gods through song. This statement earned her an avalanche of criticism from the media and civil society and provoked radical Hindu elements to undertake a smear campaign against her (Rana 2014). She has said that she simply ignores the retaliation. Many continue to admire her contributions to the music world in Nepal.

Another well-known actress, Jayasudha, was born to Hindu parents but converted to Christianity in 2001. She stated that she found Jesus after suffering a water-related accident. She has not faced any pressure due to her conversion (Joy Foundations 2015). Similarly, another actress, Nagma, born of a Muslim father and Hindu mother, experienced no pressure when she declared her faith in Christ (Mundaplamoodu 2017).

Anand Mahadevan, a well-known journalist in India, and his wife are believers in Christ. They are Brahmins in the Indian caste system. Mrs. Mahadevan goes by her Hindu name. Her faith in Jesus continues with no pressure (Mahadevan 2008).

2.1.3 Female Christian converts afflicted due to their faith

There are 33 pressure points in the lives of Christian women under pressure for their faith (Fisher and Miller 2018:5). The Religious Liberty Commission indicated in its report for 2018 that targeting of minorities, Dalits and women by anti-Christian fanatical forces had visibly increased; the report also listed 26 events in which women were afflicted in various ways (Religious Liberty Commission of the Evangelical Fellowship of India 2019). For example, on 29 April 2018, a mob of more than 25 radicals disrupted Full Gospel Pentecostal Church and assaulted five women in Baburia Kheda, Raebareli district in Uttar Pradesh.

Sarita, a Christian convert in central India, met and married Mohan, a Hindu. She had to experience brutality and physical and mental torment from her husband for her faith in the Lord Jesus for 13 years. She was eventually abandoned by her husband and left to raise her two children by herself.

Another report stated, "A mob had attacked around seventy believers on 24 February 2019; women in the congregation were being beaten and dragged by their hair, while they were worshipping the Lord in the state of Maharashtra" (Persecution Relief 2019b).

A 2019 report indicated that a pastor and her congregation were assaulted during a Sunday worship service, in a religiously motivated attack in Barwala, Panchkula district of Haryana, involving a mob of 20 thugs (Persecution Relief 2019a).

A pregnant woman and her five children were thrown out of their village by her husband and in-laws after she refused to renounce her Christian faith (World Watch Monitor 2018).

2.1.4 Context differentiates the extent of persecution

Based on the different incidents presented, it can be concluded that the presence and extent of persecution against Christian women depends on where and in what context they live. Relevant factors include the region of India where the person resides, the religious faith of the other family members in the house, and how the converted person expresses her faith. Christian women living in provinces where religious secularism is predominant have a lower likelihood of experiencing persecution than those in a province where religious fanaticism is strong.

2.1.5 The church's response to persecution

The church in India is a large and powerful force. Many Christian associations, such as the Religious Liberation Commission of the Evangelical Fellowship of India, All India United Christian Front, Christian Council of India, United Christian Forum for Human Rights, All India Christian Minority Front, Catholic Secular Forum and others have been responding to the present adverse context. Most of them have blamed Hindu fundamentalists for all kinds of attacks on churches.

As one form of response to the persecution, about 10,000 Christians in eastern India's Jharkhand state formed a 20-kilometer human chain to protest what they called the state-sponsored harassment of Christians and a hate campaign against them (Thomas 2018). In addition, some 20,000 Christians from various denominations filled roads in at least 16 cities and towns, shouting slogans against government inaction with regard to anti-Christian activities allegedly carried out by upper-caste Hindu groups in Coimbatore on 17 April 2018 (Christian Today 2018). The Synod of Pentecostal Churches in Tamil Nadu organized protests in reaction to at least 15 cases of violence against Christians in the first three months of 2018 (Voice of South Asia 2018).

Some agencies offer assistance to the persecuted Christians, pastors and churches; however, details of their services and accomplishments are unknown or unpublished. In most cases, these actions do not address directly the particular forms of persecution and violence experienced by women.

3. Exploring the causes of persecution of female converts

In light of the divergent experiences of religious converts, one cannot conclude that faith in Jesus Christ is the sole cause of the pressures that many female Christian converts undergo in India. Theoretically, faith in Jesus should not be an issue, as Hindu tradition allows "Hinduism to accommodate all other religious communities, with their own gods, beliefs, and practices" (Hiebert 2004:325). The ethos of Hinduism is expressed in the phrase "Ekam Sat, Viprah Bahudda Vadanti," which means "There is an eternal Truth, but there are many ways to achieve it" (Hindu Vivek Kendra n.d.). For this reason, many converts do not face pressure from surrounding Hindus.

The following subsections discuss some of the fundamental but not always obvious reasons why female Christian converts do face pressure, as derived from publications and first-hand sources.

3.1 Fighting over membership gains and losses

Encounters between different religions give rise to competition over the gain and loss of adherents that occur when some people reject the teachings of one religion and accept those of another. This battle generates tensions, conflicts and violence between religious groups, especially in a nation like India, which is democratic but has not firmly established secular governance. Globally, conversion in general is considered provocative, and thus precautionary measures to prevent conversions have been taken by various non-Christian religions.

Within the Indian context, forces of religious nationalism have set forth an agenda for a nationalized religion (Hinduism) to gain political prominence. These forces intentionally breed threats against Christians to suppress their growth in order to win the political favour of Hindus. Hindu fundamentalism grew over long years of resentment stirred in the hearts of Hindus by intolerant Islamic invaders and European Christian colonizers (Shullai 2017). Muslim atrocities and Christian conversions during the colonial period generated resentment, anger, fear and defiance in Hindus toward non-Hindus (Wink 2002). This continued even after the nation's independence. The trend is exacerbated by the present political power wielded by Hindu fundamentalists.

3.2 Retaliation towards extraction

In the process of religious conversion, the practices of some evangelical groups cause cultural, custom-related and family clashes. Extraction of women from long years of identity and customary beliefs and practices and their replacement by a new and alien Christian identity make Hindus and the Hindutva[3] community angry and bitter towards Christian converts.

3.3 Misperceptions

Astrid Lobo Gajiwala (1998), a Christian activist who writes regularly on Christian issues, asked her Hindu husband and other educated Hindu friends why so many people express anger about people's religious conversions. She described her findings in this way: "They just don't see Christians as Indians; they see us as an alien 'other,' minions of a white Christian world that is synonymous with spiritual and racial chauvinism. Our cathedrals, our culture, and our worship set us apart." Conversion is a threat for them as it is considered a renunciation of Hindus' cultural and spiritual heritage for the purpose of adopting a Westernized religious identity.

3.4 External responses of converts

Conversion encounters in India do not merely involve a sinner's prayer, but a conscious 'response ... to the invitation, love, and work of God in Christ' (Cawley 2016:165). Internal and external elements are involved in the conversion process; belief, repentance, assurance of forgiveness, and devotion are internal components, whereas baptism, church affiliation, and participating in evangelism and mission are external and openly visible ways of acting out one's faith. Such responses usually generate pressures on new female converts especially.

---

[3] The Hindutva ideology contends that the Indian nation is nothing but the physical and emotional outcome of Hindu aspirations. The question of identity for them, therefore, is naturally settled in favour of a clearly delineated Hindu identity, while Muslims and Christians are 'outsiders' and can be considered part of India only if they accept the national culture (I. Sharma 2015:4).

3.5 Frigid relationships between religions

Misconceptions of Christians about other religions and vice versa, unfavourable propaganda produced by other religions, and other mutually offensive acts have strained the relationship between Christian and non-Christian religions. Increasing religious intolerance is another factor. A 2016 report by the U.S. Commission on International Religious Freedom cited deteriorating religious tolerance and increasing violence in India (PTI 2016). As non-Christians see the number of Christians growing in India, existing bitterness and fury can become manifested in pressures on new female converts.

3.6 A spirit of patriarchalism

Though numerous positive changes have occurred among women, chronic social issues such as gender inequality and bigotry keep many women trapped in a second-class status. One common manifestation of these problems in India is domestic violence; many other women are subject to discrimination and pressure relating to their family members' religious affiliation.

For example, Ravi, an alcoholic Hindu husband, brutally abused his wife, Rani, when she became a Christian and was baptized without his knowledge. Given his low view of women driven by his patriarchalism, his wife's personal decision to become a Christian was unacceptable to him, even though he himself believes that Jesus is one of the gods and he said he did not oppose Rani's faith in Jesus.

3.7 Unethical practices of mission agencies

The practice of unethical mission methods (Ariyarajah 2015:172) and conversion efforts by certain agencies, churches and individuals is undeniable (Bird 2016:298). Post-conversion practices that extract women converts from their families, as well as psychological or material inducements that agencies offer to women in vulnerable population sectors, trigger anger among Hindus and fanatics. This anger results in pressure against converts – particularly women, who tend to convert in greater numbers than men.

3.8 Other factors

Some other less noticeable factors can contribute to unfortunate situations. Parentally arranged marriages can negatively impact first-generation Christian believers. One young lady, the first Christian in her family, accepted Christ in September 2005, but was compelled to marry a man from her former faith. Her life turned out to be miserable, as her husband was one of the leading anti-Christian fanatics in his region. Eventually, their marriage fell apart.

In other cases, anti-Christian employers pressure female Christian employees. For example, a middle-age, married Christian woman, a recipient of a best-teacher award from the President of India, works in a school owned and managed by a Hindu company. Accordingly, she is expected to adhere to the school owners' religious beliefs, values and practices. She declines to adhere to some of them due to her Christian faith, resulting in intentional humiliation by her employer. Other Hindu teachers influence students to behave rebelliously towards her.

4. Suggestions to counter persecution

Having described a variety of apparent or plausible causes of persecution, I now turn briefly to a biblical understanding of violence and persecution. This can help to provide a nuanced understanding of persecution and how we should respond to it.

4.1 A biblical understanding of violence and persecution

Religious persecution is a painful reprisal against a community or group of communities that is viewed as impinging upon the values of the faith and practices of another religious community (Ramachandran 2010:333).

Persecution against Christians can serve in a wonderful way to build up believers in their individual faith, as well as to strengthen the church. God designed the church to function as the salt and light of the world and he sent His people into the world as lambs sent among wolves. Hence, persecution and the Christian life are interwoven. Persecution of the church is a predicted reality and a payment that disciples of the Lord Jesus are expected to offer as a mark of their commitment to the Word.

On the other hand, religious violence against adherents of the Christian religion is a brutal outcome of the animosity of certain intolerant segments of non-Christian religions. This animosity could, at times, be valid from human and ethical perspectives; even so, it still is often deemed irrational. Wars of religion are not uncommon occurrences. Today's religious violence against Christian settlements is nothing but an undeclared religious war by certain fanatical communities of Hinduism. Political power triggers religious violence (Ramachandran 2010:334).

As one biblical example of religiously oriented violence with a complex background, the violently enraged Herod, who was Idumean by origin and foreign in race and faith to the Romans, used his authority to call for the brutal killing of young babies for his own safety and to secure himself against a presumed rival. Though enmity towards Israel was bred in his bones due to his place of birth, his bloody and barbarous work was not intended as persecution of the Jews for their messianic hope. It was not persecution on account of the community's beliefs, but rather religious violence by an Edomite against the Jewish community.

To differentiate between persecution and violence, it is important to consider the meaning of the word "persecution" in the New Testament. The Holy Spirit used two key words in the New Testament, *dioko* and *thlipsis,* to distinguish between faith-related persecution and eschatology-related afflictions. There are 44 occasions of the word *dioko* in the New Testament; on 31 occasions both the King James Version and the New American Standard Bible (NASB) translate the word as persecution. The contexts of most uses of this word are exclusively related to believers experiencing pain due to their faith in the Lord. Persecution, in these cases, is the systematic attempt to suppress or to exterminate Christianity by social pressure to the point of violence (Harrison 1978:403).

Thlipsis is translated in the NASB as affliction 14 times, afflictions (plural) 6 times, anguish once, distress twice, persecution once, tribulation 16 times, tribulations 4 times and trouble once. The use of this word is mostly in the context of eschatological predictions. *Thilpsis* does not necessarily imply a hostile outcome due to someone's faith in the Lord Jesus, as *dioko* does.

Mark 4:17 exemplifies the distinction between *thlipsis* and *dioko* by using both words, in the Parable of the Sower, to describe people who fall away. Mark connects *dioko* with suffering "on account of the Word," or persecution as a Christian. Premillennial believers use *thlipsis* as a technical theological term for the great tribulation of the end times, primarily for unbelievers (Richards 1985).

The New Testament thus distinguishes between persecution and tribulation. The former is mostly associated with faith-related afflictions, whereas tribulation is the common pain that both believers in the Lord Jesus and unbelievers undergo.

4.2 Suggestions

Overall, the response to this challenge by local churches has consisted of one-time events. They have not significantly prepared the congregations in dealing with persecution. To supplement existing efforts, I offer the following suggestions, which are designed to accomplish three desired results: (1) preventing the possibility of persecution, (2) preserving believers' faith in the midst of adversity, and (3) preparing the church to grow.

4.2.1 Educate Christians and churches to prevent violence and harassments

India is constitutionally described as a sovereign, secular, democratic country. Accordingly, the rights of citizens from different religions should be protected. Presently the legislative, judicial and religious atmosphere is not in favour of Christians, as the country is yielding to religious nationalism. The church's response to violence needs more prevention and less protesting as Christians are a minority population living in a pro-Hindu atmosphere.

There are four areas in which Christians and churches need to be educated:

(1) Erasing animosity against people of other faiths: Christians should be taught to pay respect to people of other faiths, not using offensive words about them and their faith and practices.

(2) Peace building with people of other faiths: Both individuals and congregations can initiate this work with others in their neighbourhood. Peace building is not exclusive to the Christian faith.

(3) Understanding of the constitutional provisions concerning "freedom of religion" and "secularism" in an unbiased manner: Christians should also be well instructed on the Indian Penal Codes related to conversion and practising one's faith.

(4) Recognizing the psychology of the opposing community among whom they need to testify to their faith. Unbelieving people are likely to be subject to three psychological trends:

(a) Inertia – being simply unresponsive to anything Christians offer. They do not want to change. It's nothing against Christians or their offer. They have a fear of making choices or of committing to anything, a phenomenon related to a resistance to change (Alos-Ferrer 2016:1).

(b) Reaction – an unpleasant motivational arousal that emerges when people experience a threat to or loss of their freely chosen behaviours. It serves as a motivator to restore one's freedom (Steindl 2015:205).

(c) Scepticism – grounded in suspicion. In religious terms, it means being suspicious of any Christian who makes approaches, his or her presentations of any kind, and his or her source itself. A person under the grip of suspicion would not yield to anything, whatever Christians say or do.

Moreover, the dynamics of conversion are a reflection of primal forces within the human personality. The id, ego and superego engage in constant conflict. Human proclivities propel persons to seek gratification of urgent and powerful desires, but culture, religion and the conscience (superego) serve as constraints (Rambo 1999:266). Understanding this psychology is useful in helping Christians to act with wisdom and be careful as they testify and demonstrate their faith in the society.

4.2.2 Edify Christians and churches to persevere in the midst of adversities

Long-suffering faith comes through perseverance. Persecution and Christian faith cannot be separated. There is an immediate need to raise a community of men and women who display faith and confidence in the Lord, as did Daniel and his three friends who persevered in the midst of acute adversities in their day.

Since faith in Christ and persecution cannot be separated, pressure on women converts is inevitable. Christians in general, but pastors and church leaders in particular, need to learn (1) the theology of suffering, (2) eschatological predictions,

(3) persecution in church history, (4) case studies of faithful victims and martyrs, and (5) biblical teaching on enduring hardships.

4.2.3 Equip Christians and churches to face adversities positively

Witnessing for Christ in the midst of adversaries demands skill and wisdom. A level of preparation is needed that has not been attempted by the church at large in India. Most military forces prepare their special troops for battle against their enemies. For example, the United States Navy offers Survival, Evasion, Resistance and Escape (SERE) training for their key commandos. Training focuses primarily on how to accomplish assignments successfully as they pass through various trying experiences in the enemy's territory. In the same way, training is also useful for the church. This training should help to make the congregation optimistic, patient, capable of endurance under hardship, wise, brave and less vulnerable.

Disaster management could be another useful type of training. In the context of the persecution of Christian women, disaster management could entail preparation for facing possible atrocities, equipping women for safe responses, and teaching them to work promptly towards recovery so as to lessen the impact.

4.2.4 Eradicate the influence of social customs, practices and patriarchal culture

The church in India in general is polarized along caste lines. As a Hindu construct, the caste system does not value all humankind equally. Historically, the church has frequently tolerated the injustices of the caste system (Raja 1999:30-31). Acceptance of the caste system should be eradicated. As a deeply-seated construct in the Indian social imagination, this cannot take place through mere teaching and writing. An intentional drive to abolish casteism among Christians should be encouraged. Christians can help to move Indian society toward this goal through supporting inter-caste marriages, non-caste identities in names, renouncing caste-based special privileges, encouraging casteless, inter-mingled community dwellings, and casteless churches.

In 2018, 90 Christian women came together to discuss the topic of gender equality in the church for two days. This event was organized by the Indian Christian Women's Movement in Pune, which had expressed concern regarding obvious gender discrimination in the churches. Churches need to educate their own people on gender issues and solutions. Since paternalism is present in Bible narratives, many Christians continue to reinforce paternalism in their own society. Understandings *of masculinity and femininity vary from culture to culture, and their boundaries are often blurry, sometimes even in the Bible. Women in the Bible are of limited normative value in a different cultural context, since* they are of necessity laden with specific cultural beliefs about gender identity and roles. Christian faith-bearers should analyse culturally situated biblical statements about men and women and their characters and roles in order to reconstruct biblical relationships between them in contemporary contexts is the ideal way. First Corinthians 11:11 and Galatians 3:28 can be a helpful start to this analysis as they suggest that men and women have equally strong personalities, combining toughness and gentleness, assertiveness and nurturing behaviour, as called for by the situation. Men and women are equally saved, equally Spirit-filled, and equally sent (Volf 1966:*181-82*).

4.2.5 Extend ministry among the afflicted women in one's region

Finally, churches can offer human resources and personal development programs for women, conduct awareness programs on welfare schemes available for women from governments and non-governmental organizations, and provide legal and counselling assistance for female victims.

5. Conclusion

Although this brief study is delimited only to Christian women in India, its suggestions are relevant to women in most countries of south and southeast Asia. It can also be relevant to patriarchal societies where Christianity is a religious minority.

Of course, the persecution of Christian women cannot be fully stopped. Since Christian faith is anchored on Christ's second coming and since seasons of suffering on the earth are part of eschatological truth, sufferings of Christians will undoubtedly continue. This paper affirms the sovereignty of God, but it also calls for human responsibility. The challenge facing Christian women in India and similar contexts is how to be strengthened by the power of the Holy Spirit and function effectively as God's witnesses (Acts 1:8; 1 Pet. 4:16). Christians have been sent like lambs among wolves; Christian women need to be wise as serpents and innocent as doves as they witness for Jesus (Matt. 10:16).

References

Alos-Ferrer, Carlos. 2016. 'Inertia and Decision Making', *Frontiers in Psychology*, 7(24), pp. 1-9.
Ariyarajah, S. Wesley. 2015. 'Conversion and Religious Freedom', in Shanta P. Premavardhana (ed.), *Religious Conversion: Religious Scholars Thinking Together*. Hoboken, NJ: Wiley Blackwell, pp. 161-76.
Bertelsmann Stiftung. 2018. *ETI 2018 Country Report: India*. Gütersloh: Bertelsmann Stiftung.
Bird, Frederick. 2016. *The Practices of Global Ethics*. Edinburgh: Edinburgh University Press.
Cawley, Luke. 2016. *The Myth of the Non-Christian*. Downers Grove, IL: InterVarsity Press.

Center for Study of Society and Secularism and Minority Rights Group International. 2017. *A Narrowing Space: Violence and Discrimination against India's Religious Minorities*, [online]. Available at: https://bit.ly/3jJqm71.
Christian Today. 2018. '20,000 Christians in TN Protest Against Violence', [online]. Available at: https://bit.ly/34BKaDc.
Fisher, Helene and Elizabeth Miller. 2018. *Gendered Persecution: World Watch List 2018 Analysis and Implications*. Open Doors International. Available at: https://bit.ly/33BxZGY.
Frykenberg, Robert Eric. 2016. 'The Legacy of Pandita Ramabai: Mahatma of Mukti', *International Bulletin of Mission Research*, 40(1), pp. 60-70.
Gajiwala, Astrid Lobo. 1998. 'Martyrdom: The Call for the New Millennium', *The Examiner*, 18 July.
Goldsmith, Belinda and Meke Beresford. 2018. 'Exclusive: India most dangerous country for women with sexual violence rife - global poll', Thomson Reuters Foundation, [online]. Available at: https://www.reuters.com/article/us-women-dangerous-poll-exclusive-idUSKBN1JM01X.
Harrison, Everett F., ed. 1978. *Baker's Dictionary of Theology*. Grand Rapids: Baker.
Hiebert, G. Paul. 2004. 'The Christian Response to Hinduism', in Hedlund, Roger E. and Paul Joshua Bhakiaraj (eds.), *Missiology for the 21st Century*. Delhi: ISPCK, pp. 324-35.
Hindu Vivek Kendra. n.d. 'A Pluralistic Hinduism', [online]. Available at: http://www.hvk.org/publications/cihp/ch1.html.
Jayawardena, Kumari. 1995. *The White Woman's Other Burden: Western Women and South Asia during British Colonial Rule*. New York: Routledge.
Joy Foundations. 2015. Sis.Jayasudha (Film Actress) Testimony – Telugu Christian Testimonies [video]. 13 March. Available at: https://www.youtube.com/watch?v=cCH7OjcSQrk.
Mahadevan, Anand. 2008. I, the Convert. *Outlook*, [online]. Available at: https://www.outlookindia.com/magazine/story/i-the-convert/238770.
Mundaplamoodu, Santhosh. 2017. Indian Film Actress Nagma Convert to Christian Testimony [video]. 28 January. Available at: https://www.youtube.com/watch?v=-GZrMDzcB30.
National Crime Records Bureau. 2013. *Crime in India: 2012 Compendium*. Ministry of Home Affairs, Government of India.
National Crime Records Bureau. 2016. *Accidental Deaths and Suicides in India, 2015*. Ministry of Home Affair, Government of India.
National Crime Records Bureau. 2017. *Crime in India: 2016 Snapshots (States/UTs)*. Ministry of Home Affairs, Government of India.
Open Doors. 2019. *World Watch List 2019*, [online]. Available at: https://bit.ly/2SQWnyt.
Pandya, Haresh. 2015. 'Sister Nirmala Joshi: Missionary of Charity', *Outlook*, [online]. Available at: https://bit.ly/34GsDd1.
PTI. 2016. 'Religious Freedom has Deteriorated in India, Says US Report; Govt Disagrees', *Indian Express*. Available at: https://bit.ly/30INICb.
Persecution Relief. 2019a. 'Pastor Sister Baljit Kaur and Congregation Assaulted During Worship Service, Haryana', *Persecution Relief Daily News*. Available at: https://bit.ly/3jI8DNf.
Persecution Relief. 2019b. 'Sunday Service Disrupted, Women and Children Beaten, Maharashtra', *Persecution Relief Daily News*. Available at: https://bit.ly/2GTnTbu.

Priya, Nanda, Gautam Abhishek, Verma Ravi, Khanna Aarushi, Khan Nizamuddin, Brahme Dhanashri, Boyle Shobhana and Kumar Sanjay. 2014. *Study on Masculinity, Intimate Partner Violence and Son Preference in India*. New Delhi: International Center for Research on Women.

Raja, Jebamalai. 1999. 'The Problem of Caste within the Church', *Dharmaram Journal of Religions and Philosophies* 24(1), pp. 28-39.

Ramachandran, Jayakumar. 2010. 'Violence in Religious Segments of India and Christian response: A Biblical and Missiological Understanding', in Fox, Frampton F. (ed.) *Violence and Peace*. Bangalore: ATA/CMC, pp. 331-356.

Rambo, Lewis R. 1999. Theories of Conversion: Understanding and Interpreting Religious Change. *Social Compass* 46(3), pp. 259-71.

Rana, Trishna. 2014. 'For God's Sake', *Nepali Times*. Available at: http://archive.nepalitimes.com/regular-columns/Here-We-Go/for-gods-sake,359.

Religious Liberty Commission of the Evangelical Fellowship of India. 2019. *Hate and Targeted Violence Against Christians in India 2018*. New Delhi: RLC.

Richards, Lawrence O. 1985. *Expository Dictionary of Bible Words*. Grand Rapids: Regency.

Robinson, Jacob. 2013. Sis.pusbalatha AVM Rajan Part 1 & 2 [video]. Available at: https://www.youtube.com/watch?v=LEWbVvSzgpw.

Saldanha, Virginia. 2016. *The Power of Religion over Women in India*. Global Sisters Report, 10 November. Available at: https://bit.ly/3lrqLvh.

Sauer, Christof and Thomas Schirrmacher, 2012. 'A Global Survey', in Taylor, William, Antonia van der Meer, and Reg Reimer (eds.), *Sorrows and Blood*, pp. 9-16. Pasadena, CA: William Carey Library.

Sharma, Indira. 2015. 'Violence against Women: Where Are the Solutions?', *Indian Journal of Psychiatry*, 57(2), pp. 131-139.

Sharma, Ratika. 2015. 'Gender Equality in India: Causes and Remedies', *International Research Journal of Management Sociology & Humanity*, 6(8), pp. 141-142.

Sharma, Jyotirmaya. 2015. *Hindutva*. Noida, Uttar Pradesh, India: Harper Collins.

Shullai, Pynhunland. 2017. 'Colonialism, Christianity and Mission Activities in India: Postcolonial Perspectives', *International Journal of Humanities and Social Science Studies*, 3(5), pp. 324-334.

Song on Fire. 2016. Actress Mohini Christian Testimony [video]. Available at: https://www.youtube.com/watch?v=TgC7Tgjk_6k.

Steindl, C., E. Jonas, S. Sittenthaler, E. Traut-Mattausch, and J. Greenberg. 2015. Understanding Psychological Reactance: New Developments and Findings. *Zeitschrift für Psychologie*, 223(4), pp. 205-214.

Storkey, Elaine. 2015. *Scars across Humanity*. London: SPCK.

Thomas, Saji. 2018. 'Thousands protest harassment of Christians in India', UCA News. Available at: https://bit.ly/3iP9nza.

Thomson Reuters Foundation. 2018. 'The World's Most Dangerous Countries for Women 2018'. Available at: https://poll2018.trust.org/country/?id=india.

Volf, Miroslav. 1966. *Exclusion and Embrace: A Theological Exploration of Identity, Otherness, and Reconciliation*. Nashville, TN: Abingdon.

Voice of South Asia. 2018. 'Unrest among Christians in India Increasing as Archbishop Calls for Prayer', [online]. Available at: https://bit.ly/3jIr6tl.

Wink, Andre. 2002. *Al-Hind, the Making of the Indo-Islamic World: Early Medieval India and the Expansion of Islam 7th-11th Centuries*. Leiden: Brill.

World Watch Monitor. 2018. 'India "World's Most Dangerous Country for Women," as Five Activists Gang-Raped', [online]. Available at: https://bit.ly/36KOu5D.

Noteworthy

The noteworthy items are structured in three groups: annual reports and global surveys, regional and country reports, and specific issues. Though we apply serious criteria in the selection of items noted, it is beyond our capacity to scrutinize the accuracy of every statement made. We therefore disclaim responsibility for the contents of the items noted. The compilation was produced by Janet Epp Buckingham.

Annual reports and global surveys

World Watch List 2016
Open Doors, World Watch Research, February 2016
http://opendoorsanalytical.org/world-watch-list-documentation/ (password: freedom) The World Watch List (WWL) represents the 50 countries where persecution of Christians is the worst and is compiled from a specially designed questionnaire of around 80 questions covering various aspects of religious freedom. The top three countries for persecution are North Korea, Iraq and Eritrea. The above is the original source and most extensive documentation for the multiple reproductions in various languages for popular use.

International Religious Freedom Report for 2016
US Department of State, August 2017
https://2009-2017.state.gov/j/drl/rls/irf/religiousfreedom//index.htm#wrapper
The US Department of State produces a comprehensive annual report on international religious freedom.

Annual Interim Report 2017
European Parliament Intergroup, EU, June 2017
http://www.religiousfreedom.eu/2017/06/20/annual-interim-report-2017/
The European Parliament Intergroup on Freedom of Religion or Belief and Religious Intolerance released its third annual report on freedom of religion or belief around the world.

United Nations Special Rapporteur Reports
Special Rapporteur on freedom of religion or belief, Heiner Bielefeldt, December 2015
https://www.ohchr.org/Documents/Issues/Religion/A-HRC-31-18_en.pdf
The UN Special Rapporteur on freedom of religion or belief issued a report, A/HRC/28/66, that focused on the relationship between the right to freedom of religion or belief and the right to freedom of opinion and expression.

Special Rapporteur on freedom of religion or belief, Heiner Bielefeldt, August 2016

https://www.ohchr.org/Documents/Issues/Religion/A-71-269_en.pdf

The UN Special Rapporteur on freedom of religion or belief issued an interim report that focused on the broad range of violations of freedom of religion or belief, their root causes and variables.

Regional and Country Reports

China: Freedom of Religion or Belief
Christian Solidarity Worldwide, October 2016

https://www.csw.org.uk/2016/10/19/report/3305/article.htm

Restrictions on the right to freedom of religion or belief continue to be a concern in China. This downward trend fits into a broader pattern of increasing human rights abuses under President Xi.

Total Denial: Violations of Religion or Belief in North Korea
Christian Solidarity Worldwide, September 2016

https://www.csw.org.uk/2016/09/22/report/3263/article.htm

CSW published a report documenting violations of the right to food, life, freedom of expression, freedom of religion or belief, freedom of movement, as well as various violations associated with prison camps.

Special issues

Report: Religious persecution and refugees 2016
Christian Solidarity Worldwide, June 2016

https://www.csw.org.uk/2016/06/23/report/3145/article.htm

Nearly 60 million people worldwide are currently displaced because of conflict, violence and persecution – the highest number since the Second World War. Violations of the right to freedom of religion or belief are one of the key reasons why people are forced to leave their countries of origin.

EU appoints first special envoy for the promotion of freedom of religion or belief
European Union, May 2016

https://ec.europa.eu/commission/presscorner/detail/en/IP_16_1670

President Jean-Claude Juncker announced his decision to appoint Mr Ján Fige (former European Commissioner for Education, Training, Culture and Youth from 2004-2009) as the first Special Envoy for the promotion of freedom of religion or belief outside the European Union.

Marrakesh Declaration protects religious minorities in Muslim countries
King Muhammad VI of Morocco, 27 January 2016
http://www.marrakeshdeclaration.org/marrakesh-declaration.html
King Muhammed VI hosted a conference in Morocco supported by the Forum for Promoting Peace in Muslim Societies, based in the UAE. At this conference, the Marrakesh Declaration was signed that sets out a legal framework for protecting religious minorities in Muslim countries.

IIRF Report on Christians in OIC countries
International Institute for Religious Freedom, 2016
https://www.iirf.eu/site/assets/files/107325/iirf_reports_2016_3.pdf
The IIRF published a report written by Thomas Schirrmacher, *The member States of the Organisation of the Islamic Cooperation (OIC) have 300 million Christian citizens*. This is a Commentary based on a table of member countries of the OIC and the religion of their citizens – a statistical research project of the International Institute of Religious Freedom (2013, translated 2016).

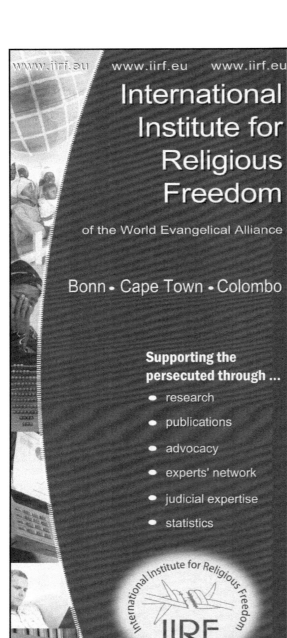

Book Reviews

Women, Religion, and Peacebuilding: Illuminating the Unseen
Susan Hayward and Katherine Marshall (eds.)
Washington: United States Institute of Peace Press, 2015, 384 pp., ISBN 9781601272928, US $24.95.

This informative book addresses an information gap on the intersection between women of faith and peacebuilding. Women are marginalized in peacebuilding in general, and religious women even more so. Yet many religious women engage in peacebuilding animated by their faith.

The experience of women in situations of war and conflict mirrors the experience of women persecuted for their faith. Sexual violence is often perpetrated against women as an element of war. As men participate as combatants, women are thrust into new economic roles, often becoming the family breadwinners. Following a conflict, women are expected to resume a more traditional role, frequently resulting in domestic conflict and the re-marginalization of women.

The role of religious women in these situations is complex. Their religious tradition often affirms a traditional role for women, yet their religious teachings encourage them to work for peace in their communities. Violent conflict can provide opportunities for these women leaders to take public roles in working towards peace. These roles can include witness, educator, advocate, mediator or direct actor.

The book is divided in two parts, the first focusing on the distinctive approaches of different religious traditions and the second providing case studies from these different religions. Catholics, Muslims, Buddhists, Hindus and Jews are covered. The case studies describe peacebuilding efforts in several high-profile conflict situations, including Indonesia, Bosnia and Herzegovina, Israel and Nigeria.

The book concludes with chapters on strengthening and empowering religious women in the work of peacebuilding.

Hayward and Marshall have done a great service in shining a light on peacebuilding work, which often is hidden behind the scenes. Women's efforts are often informal and local while men take on the higher-profile work of negotiating the terms of peace. Yet women do vital work in finding the common ground within communities that is necessary for long-term peace.

This book is a valuable addition to the literature on gender and religious freedom, as religious groups are often minorities and can be subject to persecution. All the conflicts covered in the book have religious aspects and gave rise to allegations of persecution on the basis of religion.

One frustration is that the reader is left wanting to hear more. The conflicts in Israel and Nigeria, for example, are on-going. What are women doing now in those situations? What are the stories of women of various faiths who continue to strive to be peacebuilders?

We need more books like this one, as they can build the foundations for understanding and peacebuilding that are so needed on areas of violent conflict.

Prof Dr Janet Epp Buckingham, Trinity Western University

Gender Inclusiveness: A Biblical Prescription for Enhancing the Relationship of Men and Women
Adamu Bakoshi

Jos, Nigeria: Challenge Press, 2019, 191 pp., ISBN 9781375183, US$ 5.

This book, written by a Nigerian pastor, seems like a breath of fresh air coming from a country that is known for gendered persecution. Bakoshi advocates for gender inclusiveness, recognizing that African patriarchy requires "balancing." He believes that gender has been used as a weapon for oppression and that the church must "speak up and act for gender justice and freedom."

Bakoshi begins by defining gender inclusiveness as "the perspective of biblical equality or egalitarianism. It is the no-holds bar on women's participation in all spheres of life and church" (2). In his book, he takes a biblical approach and a womanist angle, hoping to inspire the church to intentionally engage with society where its treatment of gender issues is contrary to the Bible.

Bakoshi believes that "biblical content and exegetical methodology should determine praxis" (14) and ends each chapter with a clear suggestion as to what one should do. He firsts looks at the creation story of Genesis 1–3 and then proceeds to outline the patriarchal gender structures in the Old Testament and how women were treated in the New Testament.

Bakoshi illustrates Jesus' esteem and respect for women as equal to men: he conversed and interacted with them regardless of their gender and social standing. He also incorporated women's perspectives in his teachings, such as his reference to a hen desiring to gather her chicks under her wings (Mt 25:37; Lk 13:34). Bakoshi then discusses controversial texts from Paul's letters and concludes by exhorting the church to remember its identity as a new community of God.

In his biblical exegesis, Bakoshi does not simply choose between the established complementarian and egalitarian approaches, preferring to let the exegesis guide him. This approach leads at times to a tension-filled position, one that he believes is possible as the tension of "good and evil is everywhere one turns" (7). As an example, he believes that Genesis 1 supports gender inclusiveness in all spheres of life, private and public. At the same time, because of the fall as described in Genesis 3, he argues that it is better for a woman to submit to her husband to maintain a harmonious union.

A large section of the book is dedicated to passages regarding women in Paul's letters, including 1 Corinthians 11:2-16; Galatians 3:28; Ephesians 5:22-23; Colossians 3:18-19; 1 Timothy 2:11-15 and 3:11. In his exegesis, Bakoshi provides nuanced, detailed interpretations with significant implications for today. For example, he argues that gender distinction is part of one's ontology and should therefore be respected in today's postmodern world.

In the final chapter, Bakoshi reminds the reader that "the church's bickering over gender is often times blocking the mission of the church. Christ is not interested in our roles but in our transformation as his children" (133). For him, "there should be that freedom for all members of the community of God to live up to their calling of God. Whomever God calls, man or woman, he equips through the gift of the Holy Spirit to carry out that assignment" (133). This Christian God is not territorial but the God of all people. To fulfil its calling as God's community, the church should develop well-rounded personalities to lead the church. In this way, gender discrimination can be ended.

This book is a valuable resource for pastors and others who desire to reduce gender discrimination, especially in African churches.

Dr Peirong Lin, Research Coordinator, Theological Concerns Department, World Evangelical Alliance

Religious Freedom at Risk: The EU, French Schools, and Why the Veil was Banned
Melanie Adrian

Berlin: Springer, 2016, 189 pp., ISBN 9783319362298, 71.39 .

Melanie Adrian took a unique approach to analysing the experience of the Muslim minority in France: she moved into their neighbourhood and taught at their school. This is all the more unusual because Adrian is Canadian. By becoming part of a banlieu school outside Paris, Adrian gained the trust of local students, particularly women, and learned their stories about being a marginalized minority in France. As one of the women says, "Being Muslim in France is like being defiled. You are obligated to always prove to people that you have value while everyone else already does" (149).

Adrian reviews the European Court of Human Rights' jurisprudence on wearing the hijab. The Court grants states a "margin of appreciation" to make rules on inclusion of religion in the public square. Thus, states such as Turkey and France have been able to ban wearing the veil at schools and universities.

France has tried to 'solve' the problem of Muslims being a ghettoized minority first by banning the wearing of "conspicuous religious symbols" in 2004 and then by banning the hijab in 2011. The impetus for these actions derived first from the 11 September 2001 attacks in the United States and then from Muslim riots in the banlieu of Paris in 2005. Adrian details this history in chapter 4 of the book.

But hijab-wearing women have never been the people involved in violence. France has therefore focused on what Muslim women wear in public rather than addressing issues related to the young Muslim men who are engaged in violence.

At the heart of this book, chapter 5 explains why Muslim women wear the hijab and how doing so affects their daily lives. As Adrian surmises, inside their communities, the hijab protects women and is seen as a sign of religious devotion, but in the rest of French society, wearing the hijab is a sign of otherness (135).

Adrian thoroughly canvasses the reasons why Muslim women may choose to wear the hijab. She details the public discussions that led to restrictions on wearing it at schools. She also addresses the public debates over this issue, which were often characterized by stereotypical understandings of Muslim women.

The final chapter considers the meaning of "integration." Much of the justification for banning the hijab is the desire to help Muslim immigrants from North Africa to integrate into French society. Adrian surmises that "integration" is synonymous with pushing Muslims to privatize their religion and assimilate into the dominant secular culture.

The hijab is a flashpoint, a very visible symbol of Muslim identity. It has been an issue in many countries, including Muslim-dominant countries such as Turkey. The narratives in this book represent similar situations in other countries as well.

Christians will recognize their own communities in the stories French Muslims tell about suspicion, marginalization and discrimination. Minority groups commonly experience being viewed with suspicion by a dominant culture that is secular or of a different religion. The pressure to assimilate is very similar all over the world.

This book is a helpful addition to the literature on women's experiences of religious persecution.

Prof Dr Janet Epp Buckingham, Trinity Western University

Surviving the forgotten Armenian genocide: a moving personal story
Smpat Chorbadjian, ed. Patrick Sookhdeo

McLean, Virginia: Isaac Publishing: 2015, 123 pp., ISBN 978-0991614578, paperback, US $10.

The centenary of the Armenian genocide has brought renewed attention to this sad event. The quip attributed to Hitler, "Who, after all, speaks today of the annihilation of the Armenians?" can now be definitively answered. Patrick Sookhdeo and Isaac Publishing have contributed to this awareness by making available the remarkable chronicle of Smpat Chorbadjian, a refugee who witnessed some of the worst of the deportations and killings and yet survived to record his experiences before undergoing a deeper conversion to Christian faith. The account is compelling, disturbing and inspiring.

Chorbadjian's account and Sookhdeo's commentary make it clear that, although matters of political expediency were involved and although the Armenians were targeted in part because of their ethnicity, they also suffered because they were Christians. Sookhdeo justifies the term "genocide" by describing the violence as "orchestrated" and the result of a "centrally planned strategy."

Some 200,000 people managed to save themselves by converting to Islam, though this was not a certain route to protection either. The chronicle testifies that some Muslims disapproved of the deportations and courageously helped the Armenian Christians.

But the purpose of this book is not simply to elicit righteous indignation or fan polemical flames; quite the opposite. Without minimizing or excusing the atrocities in any way, Sookhdeo ends the story by setting forth one scholarly interpretation that is highly salutary for today. He suggests that the atrocities may have resulted from political fears by Turkish authorities in the preceding decades – fears that were exacerbated by Western humanitarian pressure.

According to this view, the Armenians had endured a second-class status within the Ottoman Empire "quietly and uncomplainingly." However, Western intervention in circumstances that were "unjust but stable" both raised nationalist expectations among the Armenians and incited concerns among the Turkish authorities that a foreign Christian presence was a political threat, perhaps a fifth column for outside power ambitions. Ignorance of Islamic fears of "humiliation" by the West also contributed to the situation: "The West's good intentions tragically backfired and made the situation of the Armenians immeasurably worse than before; even more tragically, the West did nothing to intervene and stop the killing that they had inadvertently triggered."

Such an interpretation places a heavy burden on us to consider our complicity in unintended consequences. But understanding offers the hope of learning from mistakes, and this lesson might be applied in many circumstances today. Self-righteousness seldom helps anyone. In this case, the tragic interaction of liberal humanitarianism and authoritarian reality may make the Armenian genocide a precursor for the unprecedented death and destruction the world has experienced in the century since then.

Dr Stephen Baskerville, Patrick Henry College

Nations under God: The geopolitics of faith in the twenty-first century

Luke M. Herrington, Alasdair McKay, and Jeffrey Haynes (eds.)

Bristol, UK: E-International Relations, 2015, 296 pp., ISBN 978-1910814048 (paperback), 978-1910814062 (e-book), free download.

Scholars of international relations have 'got religion.' Pointing out religion's importance in international affairs has become a publishing industry. But as the editors of this work are the first to insist, religion has in fact been intertwined with diplomatic politics throughout history. So what is so novel about this newfound interest?

The principal bête noire of this new generation of scholars is secularization theory, a fashionable trend during the 1960s and 1970s that consisted largely of academically belabouring what, in the popular climate of the time, seemed obvious: "that religion would gradually fade in importance and cease to be significant via modernity's seemingly unyielding forces," as the introduction by Luke M. Herrington and Alasdair McKay summarizes it. Or in the words of sociologist Bryan Wilson, secularization is "the process whereby religious thinking, practice, and institutions lose their social significance."

This fashion, which once seemed so incontrovertible, now looks foolish in view of the resurgence of political conflict driven by fanatical religion, plus more moderate versions. So far, however, the new religious awareness sometimes hardly seems to go beyond elaborate exercises in pointing this out, to the point where we may now be in danger of kicking a dead dog.

One may also wonder why secularization theorists continue to shape the discussions, if only with their mea culpas. No shortage of scholars tried to call our attention to religion's critical importance all along, and they were ignored and relegated to obscurity. Why are their works not dusted off and university places made available to them, since they were right all along? Such are the casualties of academic fashion.

The generalized nature of the recent counter-trend is reflected in the broad, theoretical approach of many essays in this book. Despite ruminations on such abstract questions as "What is religion?" one result is to lump together Islamist terrorism with, for example, Christian advocacy groups in Western democracies because they are both 'religious' – a device that, whether intentionally or not, rationalizes certain polemic purposes, among them the blaming of all religion for the acts of extremists. Abstract theorizing also risks perpetuating and exacerbating the separation of scholarship from reality that created the mistakes in the first place.

But this collection presents a range of approaches, all helpfully short and thus useful for classroom use. The best consist of case studies that offer practical information about particular manifestations. Herrington and McKay's introduction presents a highly informative overview of the problems and debates. Stephen Dawson's essay then succinctly summarizes about as much theory as is necessary for most readers. John Rees provides useful information on the important case of Egypt. Ruy Llera Blanes gives an interesting short overview of religious politics in Angola. Kaarina Aitamurto's study of Russian paganism is a not as marginal as it may appear. Ishtiaq Ahmed provides a short and reasonably complete introduction to religious conflict and freedom in Pakistan. Shireen Hunter's concise and sensible essay on the Islamic State may be the best in the book and is especially useful for teaching.

The essays specifically on religious freedom are mixed. Nilay Saiya naively accepts the Arab Spring as an unmixed blessing and fails to engage with the many commentators who blame it for unleashing horrendous persecutions and violence against religious minorities and others. Perhaps most seriously, he does not question how far the assumptions driving such policies remain operative among Western policymakers today and what the consequences will be for persecuted religious minorities. Dan Cox offers empirical data to corroborate Thomas Farr's argument connecting religious diversity and peace, though Cox's tendency to explain religious violence in terms of "lack of meaningful inclusion ... in the political process and a lack of economic opportunity and development" must be treated with suspicion.

Brent Nelsen and James Guth give a helpful introduction to the role of Christianity and the religious tensions involved in the formation of the European Union. Jonathan Benthall's short survey of efforts to encourage liberal Muslims is limited by its length. More detail on this important topic would probe some critical distinctions more thoroughly and with more nuance, as (for example) Patrick Sookhdeo and Stephen Ulph have done elsewhere.

Elizabeth Shakman Hurd offers a peculiar case study on the Sahrawi refugees in Algeria, the point of which is unclear, and the essay degenerates into gibberish. It appears to be a polemic against religious freedom, but the prose is so encumbered with impenetrable jargon that it is impossible to decipher.

Any book of this breadth on such an important topic that is available free of charge must be applauded. But it does not claim to be exhaustive. Instructors will want to be selective in assigning these essays, which can supplement more standard works like those of Brian Grim and Thomas Farr. Fortunately, most essays have copious references to other research.

Dr Stephen Baskerville, Patrick Henry College

Guidelines for authors
Version 2020-1 (February 2020)

This document combines essential elements of the editorial policy and the house style of IJRF which can be viewed on www.iirf.eu.

Aims of the journal

The IJRF aims to provide a platform for scholarly discourse on religious freedom and religious persecution. The term persecution is understood broadly and inclusively by the editors. The IJRF is an interdisciplinary, international, peer reviewed journal, serving the dissemination of new research on religious freedom and contains research articles, documentation, book reviews, academic news and other relevant items.

Editorial policy

The editors welcome the submission of any contribution to the journal. All manuscripts submitted for publication are assessed by a panel of referees and the decision to publish is dependent on their reports. The IJRF subscribes to the Code of Best Practice in Scholarly Journal Publishing, Editing and Peer Review of 2018 (https://sites.google.com/view/assaf-nsef-best-practice) as well as the National Code of Best Practice in Editorial Discretion and Peer Review for South African Scholarly Journals (http://tinyurl.com/NCBP-2008) and the supplementary Guidelines for Best Practice of the Forum of Editors of Academic Law Journals in South Africa. As IJRF is listed on the South Africa Department of Higher Education and Training (DoHET) "Approved list of South African journals", authors linked to South African universities can claim subsidies and are therefore charged page fees.

Submission adresses

- Book reviews or suggestion of books for review: bookreviews@iirf.eu
- Noteworthy items and academic news: noteworthy@iirf.eu
- All other contributions: research or review articles, opinion pieces, documentation, event reports, letters, reader's response, etc.: editor@iirf.eu

  IJRF, POBox 1336, Sun Valley 7985, Rep South Africa

Selection criteria

All research articles are expected to conform to the following requirements, which authors should use as a checklist before submission:

- **Focus:** Does the article have a clear focus on religious freedom / religious persecution / suffering because of religious persecution? These terms are understood broadly and inclusively by the editors of IJRF, but these terms clearly do not include everything.

> **Scholarly standard:** Is the scholarly standard of a research article acceptable? Does it contribute something substantially new to the debate?
> **Clarity of argument:** Is it well structured, including subheadings where appropriate?
> **Language usage:** Does it have the international reader, specialists and non-specialists in mind and avoid bias and parochialism?
> **Substantiation/Literature consulted:** Does the author consult sufficient and most current literature? Are claims thoroughly substantiated throughout and reference to sources and documentation made?

Submission procedure

1. Submissions must be complete (see no.6), conform to the formal criteria (see no. 8-10) and must be accompanied by a cover letter (see no.3-4).
2. The standard deadlines for the submission of academic articles are 1 February and 1 August respectively for the next issue and a month later for smaller items such as book reviews, noteworthy items, event reports, etc.
3. A statement whether an item is being submitted elsewhere or has been previously published must accompany the article.
4. Research articles will be sent to up to three independent referees. Authors are encouraged to submit the contact details of 4 potential referees with whom they have not recently co-published. The choice of referees is at the discretion of the editors. The peer-review process is a double blind process. This means that you should not consult with or inform your referees at any point in the process. Your paper will be anonymized so that the referee does not know that you are the author. Upon receiving the reports from the referees, authors will be notified of the decision of the editorial committee, which may include a statement indicating changes or improvements that are required before publication. You will not be informed which referees were consulted and any feedback from them will be anonymized.
5. Should the article be accepted for publication, the author will be expected to submit a finalized electronic version of the article.
6. Include the following:
> An abstract of no more than 100 words.
> Between 3 and 10 keywords that express the key concepts used in the article.
> Brief biographical details of the author in the first footnote, linked to the name of the author, indicating, among others, year of birth, the institutional affiliation, special connection to the topic, choice of UK or American spelling, date of submission, full contact details including phone number and e-mail address.
7. Authors are expected to also engage with prior relevant articles in IJRF, the Religious Freedom Series, and IIRF Reports (www.iirf.eu) to an appropriate degree. So check for relevant articles as the peer reviewers will be aware of these.

8. Articles should be spell-checked before submission, by using the spellchecker on the computer. Authors may choose either 'UK English' or 'American English' but must be consistent. Indicate your choice in the first footnote.
9. Number your headings (including introduction) and give them a hierarchical structure. Delete all double spaces and blank lines. Use as little formatting as possible and definitely no "hard formatting" such as extra spaces, tabs. All entries in the references and all footnotes end with a full stop. No blank spaces before a line break.
10. Research articles should have an ideal length of 4 000 words and a maximum of 6 000 words. Articles longer than that are not normally accepted, but may be published if, in the views of the referees, it makes an exceptionally important contribution to religious freedom.
11. Research articles are honoured with two complimentary printed copies.
12. For research articles by members of the editorial team or their relatives, the full editorial discretion is delegated to a non-partisan editor and they are submitted to the same peer review process as all other articles.

Style requirements

1. IJRF accepts any consistently used citation style that is clearly defined named by the author. The historical citation style of the journal is the 'name-date' method (or Harvard system) for citations in the text.
2. In the Harvard Style, a publication is cited or referred to in the text by inserting the author's last name, year and page number(s) in parentheses, for example (Mbiti 1986:67- 83). More detailed examples can be found on: www.iirf.eu > journal > instructions for contributors.
3. Graphics (e.g. graphs, tables, photographs) will only be included in an article if they are essential to understanding the text. Graphics should not be included in the body of the article. Number graphics consecutively, save each in a separate file and indicate clearly in the text where each should be placed.
4. Footnotes should be reserved for content notes only, unless a footnote based citation style is used. Bibliographical information is cited in the text according to the Harvard method (see 2 above). Full citations should appear in the References at the end of the article (see below).
5. References should be listed in alphabetical order of authors under the heading "References" at the end of the text. Do not include a complete bibliography of all works consulted, only a list of references actually used in the text.
6. Always give full first names of authors in the list of references, as this simplifies the retrieval of entries in databases. Keep publisher names short.

Subscriptions (for print version only!) 2017

Please note that the IJRF is *freely available on the web* a few weeks after publication at: www.iirf.eu and you can register for an email alert.

Annual subscription fee 2017 (2 issues): **South African Rand 300**
Date: _____ VAT and postage included.

Name	
Address	
Postal/Zip Code	
Country	
Telephone	
Mobile	
Fax	
Email	

I/we wish to order *International Journal for Religious Freedom* starting with the year: 2017.

Please tick the appropriate ☐ This is a new subscription ☐ This is a renewal

☐ I/ we order the following **back issues** at Rand 150 per copy:

(NB: There was only one pilot issue in 2008)

☐ 1-1 (2008) ☐ 2-1 (2009) ☐ 2-2 (2009) ☐ 3-1 (2010) ☐ 4-1 (2011) ☐ 4-2 (2011)
☐ 5-1 (2012) ☐ 5-2 (2012) ☐ 6-1/2 (2013) ☐ 7-1/2 (2014) ☐ 8-1/2 (2015) ☐ 9-1/2 (2016)

☐ I have made an **electronic transfer** to the following account
(International: charge "all fees to sender" and add 5% for South African bank fees.)

☐ **Main Account South Africa:** Payment must be in Rand

International Institute for Religious Freedom Cape Town **Account Number** 071 117 431
Bank Standard Bank **Type of Account** Current Account
Branch Sea Point **SWIFT Code** SBZAZAJJ
Branch Code 02 41 09 **Beneficiary reference** IJRF, Year, Name

☐ **For European Customers** (in Euro) **Bank:** Volksbank Worpswede e.G., Germany
International Institute for Religious Freedom (SA) **IBAN:** DE71291665680009701200
Account Number: 9701200 **BIC:** GENODEF1WOP
Bank Code/BLZ: 29166568 **Beneficiary reference** IJRF, Year, Name

---

☐ I have paid via **GivenGain**: http://iirfct.givengain.org **(preferred for international subscriptions); payment must be in RAND).**

☐ I enclose a cheque/postal order to the value of _____ ZAR made payable to International Institute for Religious Freedom Cape Town **(For foreign cheques add R 200 for bank charges).**

Return this form with your (proof of) payment to: subscriptions@iirf.eu

IJRF, P.O. Box 1336, Sun Valley, 7985, Rep South Africa

Order Form for AcadSA Publications
Religious Freedom Series

Title	Unit Price*	Copies	Amount
Re-examining Religious Persecution: Constructing a Theological Framework for Understanding Persecution. Charles L Tieszen. Religious Freedom Series, Vol 1	R 90		
Suffering, Persecution and Martyrdom: Theological Reflections. Christof Sauer and Richard Howell (editors). Religious Freedom Series, Vol 2	R 250		
		Total	

*Prices exclude shipping and handling.
Bulk discounts on request

Personal Details

Name _____ Surname _____

Postal Address _____ Postal Code _____

Country _____

Telephone _____ E-Mail _____

Email, Fax or post this form to
AcadSA, P.O. Box 15918, Panorama, Parow 7506, Rep. South Africa
Tel: +27 21 839 1139, Fax: on request, Email: info@acadsa.co.za
www.acadsa.co.za

European Orders
Book publications of IIRF from the Religious Freedom Series and the Global Issues Series are also available in Germany from: any bookseller and most also on Amazon.